Response to *Your Spiritual Heart*

"In this book, the authenticity of McArthur's own wisdom of the heart is magnetic. He draws us into a new vision of living and then masterfully guides us down the path to realizing it. His expertise in plumbing the depths of heart intelligence is awe-inspiring."

— Rita Marie Johnson,
    author of *The Connection Practice*,
    founder The Rasur Foundation International

"Finding guidance to your spiritual heart's wisdom is a means for your soul's evolution. David has written a handbook to simplify your spiritual journey. Through his insightful stories he shares different perceptions on the choices we can make by using our brain or activating the HeartMath® process to reach and ignite your spiritual heart. The outcomes of these experiences validate the power of love through the wisdom of the heart."

— Alexandra De Avalon,
    author of *Dreaming with God*

"This book has given me the tools to gain access to my Higher Self whenever I need guidance and wisdom. The author's insights and wisdom is a true gift to anyone who picks up this book."

— Linda J. Curry,
    best-selling author of *Pebbles of Gold*

"David McArthur tells us about the importance of the spiritual heart and how activating it can serve us to induce insight, gain perspective, practice deep compassion and inspire us to act from our highest values. A must have companion for the awakening soul."

— Reverend Evelyn Foreman, M.Div.,
    author of *Power of Purpose*

"David McArthur has given me a practical way to access my own unique wisdom. Using the HeartMath® Freeze Frame® process, as refined by David, has allowed me to find answers to problems or questions that I would not have found any other way. Valuable. Practical. Elegant."

— Carl Janson

"In *Your Spiritual Heart*, David shares his personal, professional and spiritual application of these life-changing tools, as he illuminates the process of accessing heart's wisdom in ways that are vivid, vibrant, memorable and easy to apply on first reading. I highly recommend this treasure."

— Janet Carol Ryan, RScP,
HeartMath® Coach

Your Spiritual Heart

by David McArthur

Paperback ISBN: 978-1-62747-400-9
eBook ISBN: 978-1-62747-532-7

Dedicated to
Doc Childre
for his friendship and his amazing heart wisdom.
Thank you Doc.

Acknowledgements

Thank you from the depth of my heart to my wife, Kathryn. Your love has led me to my spiritual heart and inspired and sustained me there. Along this journey Tom Bird's wisdom and skill with Sabrina and his wonderful team have been guide and midwives in birthing this book. Thank you Lisa Nichols whose care brought clarity and an extra sensitivity to my manuscript.

To the crowd at HeartMath, my other family, you helped me understand my heart and let me learn and grow with you. Every one of you touched my heart in a special way. I am so very grateful. The spiritual community of Unity of Walnut Creek kept inspiring my own growth in my heart by their willingness to share their hearts with me.

As you will discover in *Your Spiritual Heart*, my family is my deepest source of heart connection. Lisa,

Peter and Anna my heart fills with gratitude for the magnificent human beings you are. Thank you for Alx, Julia and Chris who have each in their own way been a special blessing to me. Corwin, Fiona and Kirra, wow – what completely delightful and inspiring beings you are. You make my heart glow. I am so grateful to all of you for choosing me as your father and grandfather. This book is a continuation of a spiritual quest and a commitment to humankind begun with my first great teachers, Charlotte and Bruce McArthur, my parents.

Access the wisdom that manifests your heart's desire
– the right job, flow of wealth, loving relationships...
even enlightenment

Contents

Forward

It is obvious to most people that we are living in extraordinary times. Changes of all kinds are taking place faster than ever before in the history of humankind. As a result, it is an era in the evolution of our world where disruption is the constant.

It is easy to see the difficulties that disruption creates. The world's many problems are on full display. As we observe life it can be hard at times to understand and make peace with the distortions and human suffering, personal, societal and global, we see. In addition, during this disruptive phase in planetary evolution, people are often faced with extra personal challenges, many of them unexpected. It can and will get easier.

Problems and challenges often tend to draw our attention; however, I believe there is an up-side to this environment of high-speed change we are living in.

Something extraordinary and beautiful is taking place. We are growing, changing and transforming at super high speed. We are reinventing ourselves, becoming conscious co-creators fueled by self-empowered effort. Consciousness is morphing, new awareness is manifesting, psychology paradigms are shifting, systemic changes are beginning to take place and new solutions to some of our global issues are coming into view. A new, heart-based world is emerging.

At the very core of this positive momentum there is a new intelligence emerging. It is the intelligence of the heart. The intelligence of the heart embodies living more consistently from the qualities associated with heart; more love, care, compassion, appreciation, kindness and patience directing our actions. The heart's intelligence provides a doorway into our quiet presence where we can access more practical intuition. It gives us a greater ability to act on what we know and move beyond self-imposed limitations. It provides a feeling of self-security. It helps shift perceptions offering new open-ended possibilities that lead to solutions to challenges. In essence, it's heart time on the planet.

Yes "heart" has been talked about and in many ways revered for thousands of years. However, it too is evolving and a new manifestation of heart leading to a heart-based world is an evolutionary imperative of our time. That's good news. We have access to more heart-directed awareness and the ability to create a new and different life experience.

David McArthur knows this very well. His life, much like mine, has been an exploration of the heart. Throughout this book David shares his experience of finding and then listening to and following his heart. His story provides an inspirational roadmap of what is possible for each and every one of us.

As you read about David's life I'd like you to consider what the world will be like as more and more people make a deeper connection with their own hearts just as he has. What would life be like if more heart qualities, demonstrated in practical ways, were the norm rather than just random moments? What new possibilities could become real and not just future projections if the intuitive intelligence of the heart was leading the way?

The co-creation of a heart-based world starts with us. There is no need to wait. We have the capacity to experience the many benefits of activating the intelligent, spiritual heart more than ever before. Your own best friend, your heart, is knocking at your door offering comfort, a feeling of inner peace and a new sense of adventure. As we accept the heart's gifts we come to know that we have amazing power within us, at the core of our authentic self, that gives us the ability to change our lives and to influence the future of our world.

Throughout this exceptional and timely book you will be offered simple practices along with stories and examples to help you take that next step in unfolding who you truly are. As you take these next steps it's not only you who benefits. It is an important service to humanity that will in some way, seen or unseen, makes life easier for others.

Making connection with your heart simply said gives you more ability to love. My life, my growth, my heart will continue to unfold and I have more work to do in the process but at the very least I have come to know this:

The purpose of life is to love.

In the end what will matter, what will define the quality of my life and what I will have left behind, will be determined by how much I loved. I know no better way to grow my love than by living from the heart.

From My Heart to Yours With Love,
Howard

Howard Martin
Executive Vice President HeartMath® Inc.
Co-Author, *The HeartMath Solution* and *Heart Intelligence*

Introduction

This book shares my journey of discovering the amazing power, wisdom and transformation that flows through our spiritual hearts. As I share my experiences, and a few from others who also discovered their hearts' spiritual dimension, I am inviting you too to discover your spiritual heart.

What is your spiritual heart? Your spiritual heart is the expression through your physical heart of the higher aspects of your wisdom and power as a spiritual being. That wisdom and power are very real things. I'll be sharing a lot about them as we journey.

I've learned most about my spiritual heart from experiences. My journey begins with a life-altering experience of my spiritual heart, long before I understood what it was or how to access it. In the first chapters, I share that experience and the amazing situation that was the starting point of my journey of discovery.

I've come to realize that our heart's deepest desires – whether for wealth, loving relationships, a great job, career, enlightenment, happiness or all of the above – are the result of our spiritual hearts calling us to experience the fulfillment of those desires. Your spiritual heart is the only wisdom truly capable of bringing those magnificent possibilities fully into your life.

In this book, you will learn how to connect with that wisdom and power. You will learn the access code so that your heart's desires can and will be yours.

That's a pretty big promise. I distrust pie-in-the-sky promises, so I did some exploration. What I have just told you is rooted in groundbreaking science from The HeartMath® Institute, and proven in the lives of many people from all walks of life: policemen, teachers, executives, laborers, managers, caregivers, moms and others from all around the world. It works in minutes – and, as you use it, the experience of fulfillment and happiness becomes wonderfully real.

I have taught thousands of people how to access their spiritual hearts, and I have watched their lives change. Their experiences have been the greatest proof of the transformative power and wisdom that I now have the pleasure of introducing to you.

Your spiritual heart is not new to you. You have been touched by it many times. It has brought you smiles and laughter, joy beyond what you thought you could hold. It has brought you power, passion and purpose. Where life seemed darkest, you have reached for and embraced it. Sometimes you have been frightened of it. Your spiritual heart is always present in your life, although often it is difficult to identify. Its power is always available, although sometimes your spiritual heart seems difficult to access when you really need it.

This amazing power seems to be one of the most elusive things to grasp, find or discover. When we are stuck in a hard place – hurt, angry or upset – we can't even imagine that such love, care, and power could be available to us.

I understand this because it has seemed that way for me many times in my life. In those moments, if you had told me about the transforming power of my spiritual heart the way I will be telling you about it, I probably would have called you a liar and rejected as foolish idealism what I have just said to you.

Fortunately, in this journey of discovery, I proved to myself that the things I have just told you are true. We each have a spiritual heart. It is powerful. It changes us and it changes the world around us. I discovered that we actually can get to it when we are hurt, angry or afraid, if we know the access code. It is this discovery of its accessibility under duress that is one of the most meaningful discoveries to me. It is at the points of hurt and pain, fear and anger, that we most need wisdom and power. It is in those moments that we most need to express the highest qualities of our being. Those are the moments when our spiritual hearts can make the biggest difference in our lives.

In my journey of discovery, I found that I was not seeking my heart alone. Many men and women sought that connection before me. They sought this knowledge and skill across many faith traditions. They used nature, hardships, family, silence and love to try to find it. They had explored with philosophy and science.

I read some of their work, and it inspired me. However, their work could not connect me with my spiritual heart. In the end, I had to apply their discoveries. I had to experiment to see if their ways worked. I found that some of the techniques and directives I learned were wonderful and effective. Some were slightly helpful for me, and some were no help at all.

I have a background in spiritual study and service. After a legal career, I spent many years as a minister, supporting people in their spiritual growth. In this book, I am not going to go into the many ways that religious traditions try to define the spiritual heart. While they all recognize it in some way, I have found those efforts at definition can at times become barriers to experience the spiritual heart – and it is the experience that is for me the most profound.

I am relying instead on the inspiring work of science. Most of the discoveries of the heart that I will share with you are from the research of the HeartMath® Institute. The people at HeartMath® used science to map the activation of these qualities of the heart. In addition to measuring them, HeartMath® developed highly effective techniques for accomplishing the heart's transformative potential. I had the great privilege of being a part of their staff for seven years.

HeartMath® has shown us through its research how to connect directly to the heart. That direct connection is powerful, quick, and transformative. This breakthrough discovery from science lets us access the amazing wisdom of the heart. This simple discovery is to me, without a doubt, the greatest spiritual discovery of our time. It is the direct path for deep and effective spiritual connection.

While HeartMath® acknowledges the spiritual, it is in service to secular institutions such as businesses, schools, hospitals, government, police and caregivers. They come from the secular world of science and serve a secular world. While they are working with the heart, and thus have a deep and profound respect for the spiritual nature, that is not the primary focus of their books or their trainings. I get to do that.

I was the first clergy person to come across their work. I saw, in their discoveries and techniques, the practical transformative experience that was eluding so many people. With their permission, I now get to bring all of my experience of over forty years of spiritual study – including my deep involvement and appreciation of their work – to you. And I get to share this amazing discovery as the spiritual breakthrough that it is.

In this book, I am focusing primarily on the technique that HeartMath® calls Freeze-Frame®. When I am working with it, I use a different focus and describe it differently than the way they present it in their literature. I am doing this with HeartMath®'s generous permission. I call my way of working with this series of steps The Heart Wisdom Tool.

Because of my years of working closely with HeartMath®, as well as having acquired the understanding of the heart that their knowledge and skills have given me, they have very graciously allowed me an exception they do not extend to others – namely, the permission to present to you a modified version of this very effective technique. If you would like to experience their excellent research and books, many of which describe the tool Freeze-Frame®, go to www.heartmath.org or www.heartmath.com or search online for "heartmath."

Your spiritual heart is the expression through your physical heart of the higher aspects of wisdom and power that come from your spiritual self. Just as we have a physical aspect of ourselves, we also have mental, emotional and spiritual aspects of our selves. This higher spiritual nature is accessed through the physical heart. What this book focuses on is much more than a physical phenomenon or potential. It is the direct experience of your spiritual self.

I have conducted trainings, workshops and coaching all over the country, teaching people these marvelous discoveries. I've shared it with thousands of people, and many of them have found it helpful. I have often heard:

- "This really, really helped me."
- "This changed my life."
- "This makes all the difference. I needed it so much."

You, like me, have challenges in your life. Some of those challenges are very painful and difficult.

Some of the ones I will share with you were painful and difficult for me. Some of your challenges are everyday decisions and situations that you want to handle well. Some of mine were too. In both of these situations, the difficult and the everyday, your spiritual heart is there to lift you, guide you, and heal you. It has been there for me. I know it will be there for you.

Chapter 1
My Experience of My Spiritual Heart

You will discover that your spiritual heart has the power to transform your emotional conflict and turmoil into true peace in only a few minutes. It is an amazing thing to suddenly not be worried or upset after only a few moments of connecting with your spiritual heart. It really does happen. Wow, think of it – the ability to stop feeling hurt or upset whenever you want. The science will explain these startling changes that people all around the world have proven for themselves.

What do you really desire for your life? You will discover that your spiritual heart is your connection to the wisdom that is there to bring your deepest heart desires into full expression in your life. Your spiritual heart can make that happen.

Before I discovered my heart's potential, or understood anything about it, I had an experience of my spiritual heart's transformative power. It so deeply impacted me that I began a journey to discover what this power was, and to find its access code. This first experience only hinted at the wisdom and fulfillment I would eventually find through my spiritual heart.

When I first experienced the power of my spiritual heart, I did not understand what it was. What I did know was that in the greatest emotional anguish I would experience in my life, when I asked for help, I received it. I would grow to eventually understand that this response to my desperate plea was the response of my spiritual heart.

I found myself in a state of hopeless emotional turmoil. My wife Kathy – a wonderful, vibrant, beautiful, loving, caring young woman – had been murdered by a young man with a gun.

We had found each other on a blind date with one of my fellow law students. My life was suddenly transformed by her beauty and her eyes, which always held the sparkle of an indescribable, effervescent joy. This petite undergraduate, who worked in the law library at the law school I attended, became the gentle presence whose caring touch invited me out of the stupor of adolescent student into the world of meaning, sharing, caring and discovering how, through love, we could create a wonderful life together. Her love was the mystical force that helped me find my heart.

I remember one of my first glimpses into the beauty of her soul. In one of those conversations in which we explored what was important to us, she shared a memory of being a teenage girl, walking home after school with friends. One of girls in the group made fun of another girl, who was walking by herself. The girl in the group was belittling her for not being a part of an acceptable clique. Kathy shared how her heart went out to the girl, and she left her "friends" and joined the lonely girl, walking home with her and becoming her friend. Her gentle, caring heart began to show me the often-hidden beauty that kindness and thoughtfulness create in our world.

We married, and she graduated college as a teacher, eager to begin teaching young children. We were so delighted when she brought our daughter,

Lisa, into the world. Kathy had again opened a truly magical experience for me as I joined her in caring for this amazing little being – so dependent, and yet so eager to discover, explore and delight in life.

As a graduating law student, I spent a day in Santa Fe in the Governor's office, reading the bills that had been passed in the legislative session. That morning as I was leaving, with a delighted smile, Kathy said to me, "The house is full of angels." I returned home that evening, and little Lisa was standing in the crib, holding out her arms to me. I lifted her up – my heart lifted by her smile – and called to Kathy. There was no answer.

Four days of unbelievable anguish would follow. Hours of hope, on the precipice of a despair that was so dark I could not go there. Then the police chaplain came to the door. I learned that a young man we knew had passed the bounds of sanity, and with his gun, had ended this precious life.

The world I lived in had disappeared in one moment. I suddenly found myself the single parent to a precious baby girl who had just lost the center of her life, her mother. The overwhelming pain of my own loss made it difficult for me to function at the level of love and care that my little Lisa needed. The pain I felt made it difficult to function at all.

My daughter, this tiny, beautiful being, was about to have her first birthday. Her delight, her security, her joy, her whole short experience of life was her interaction with her mother. Daily she had experienced the amazing mother love that responded to each moment and experience with complete delight in caring for her. Joyously her mother had been there for her, meeting her every need.

I loved to listen as Kathy would laugh with delight and Lisa would squeal with glee. That tiny hand would reach out and touch her mommy's face, her bright eyes shining as tender arms surrounded her, holding her in the security of that deepest love. We treasured each moment − where rolling over became crawling − where each new toy was tasted, chewed and thrown. There were those tentative first steps and falls, and getting up to try again. Kathy's tender hand was always close, as steps became trips across the room, and we laughed in delight at each magnificent accomplishment. Lisa's world was filled with baths and songs, books and lullabies. Those two – again and again, moment by moment – created a world that was filled with a pure magic of the heart. It was a world that knew only care, tenderness, warmth and love.

Suddenly, that mother's love was no more. That loving embrace was not there. Her mother was gone. All the goodness this precious little being had ever known had ended.

The precious eleven-month old baby now depended on me. I had been an active part of her life, but compared to the connection and care of her mother, my presence was minor. Moreover, at that moment, it was difficult for me to function at all. I existed in a world numb with shock, which would suddenly and frequently open to wrenching emotional pain.

As I focused on my baby daughter, and reflected on her overwhelming loss, I realized what an extremely poor substitute I was for her mother. I constantly struggled to not fall into the world of anger and hatred toward the individual who ended my wife's life. I knew that this little girl who had lost everything needed her father's love, not the attention of a man struggling with anger and debilitated by loss.

I was painfully aware of this impossible conflict within me.

I had to fight each moment to not give into the anger and hatred that seemed so easy, so justified, so natural to feel. I knew that this child, in the loss of all that had been her world, her security, her happiness, needed my love and care – because I was the only one left. I knew that if I let myself be consumed with anger and hatred, I could not begin to bring to her the level of love, tenderness, understanding and patience that she so deeply needed in this moment, when her small world had been violated so deeply. So I asked for help.

My desire to care for this wonderful child, to be the daddy she needed, was a huge part of what caused me to reach into a deep place of sincerity within myself and ask for help. The pain, blame and anger it would be so easy to feel seemed so right, and so justified, that it was very difficult to even consider turning away from them. However, for my Lisa, I knew at some deep core level of my being that I had to do it. I had to find some peace, some relief from my pain and turmoil, so that I could love and care for my daughter.

I asked for help. It was not an asking to anyone or anything in the outer world. I did have caring family, both Kathy's and mine, who were there to help as they could. However, I had no concept that there was anyone or anything in the outer world that could help me with this struggle that was taking place inside of me. So my asking was within.

It could probably best be described as a form of desperate, anguished prayer. I did not even know clearly what I was asking for, because no help seemed possible. It was mostly a deeply sincere plea from the heart for help. I understood that the help I was asking for was some form of relief from the conflicting, controlling emotional world that was within me. I knew intellectually that forgiveness would have to be a part of my relief, eventually. That was a part of my asking. However, at the core of my asking was the awareness that I needed to be the loving presence that my little daughter needed. That was what was really important.

The response to my anguished asking occurred sometime in the weeks that followed. It occurred in a moment when my spiritual heart opened, although I did not understand that at the time.

I was with my delightful Lisa. We were alone in the house, playing on the floor. Having grown uncomfortable on the floor, I pushed myself up and sat on the couch. I was feeling a caring warmth in my heart for her as I watched her play on the floor before me.

Suddenly, I felt my heart expanding. I experienced an amazing, ever-growing feeling of love. It seemed to fill me, becoming so powerful that it began to overwhelm my senses. It was a love so great that I lost all awareness of anything else. I lost awareness of my daughter, of the couch, of the room. The feelings of love I experienced in that moment were greater and more powerful than any feeling, any emotion – anything I had ever experienced before or since. It filled my mind, my heart and the cells of my body. It was blissful, ecstatically blissful. It lifted me into an ecstasy that I am still completely incapable of describing. All of my awareness was filled with this overwhelming, blissful love.

Years later, a friend describing her near-death experience used the phrase, "love to the millionth power." I know she experienced what I had that day.

I have no sense of how long this experience of ecstatic love lasted. When I was able to focus my attention back on the reality of that room, Lisa was playing quietly, and I was filled with a deep, beautiful, glowing sense of peace.

In the days and weeks that followed, I discovered that the emotional conflict I had struggled with since Kathy's death no longer existed within me. I did not have to struggle to not feel anger toward the gunman. I did not feel hatred. Those feelings no longer seemed to have attractiveness to me. The struggle I had gone through to not give into that bitter world no longer existed.

Later, when I reflected on this tragedy that had filled our lives, I understood at a deep, intuitive level that the person who had taken this precious life was as much the victim of violence that had touched his life as were my wife, our little child and myself. I felt forgiveness for him and for myself. I felt peace.

It is that feeling of that amazing love, that healing of my pain, that greater wisdom from which I could now view life, that has directed my life ever since. I have searched to understand what happened to me in those moments when I was freed from the call of anger, hatred and pain.

I know that the wisdom, love and healing power I experienced in that moment on my couch, with little Lisa, is present within every one of us. It is available within you just as it was within me. I came to understand it as a power that we are able to access through our hearts. It brought me great freedom and deep peace. It is my heartfelt prayer that you let it do the same for you.

I do not want to create a false impression that I no longer struggled with the feelings of loss. Although there was a great reduction in the intensity and control that those feelings exerted on my life, they continued to be present as I genuinely sought to understand the nature of love, my love for Kathy, our love of others and the experience of loss.

The forgiveness that I desired in my asking was completely and fully given, in that experience of ecstatic love. The tortured soul who did that cruel, violent act – whom I met with in the state mental facility at a later time – evokes only compassion from my heart.

Years later, as I worked with healing emotional trauma that came up in myself or in others, I would return often to examine this core experience. It was through this that I entered an inner peace that included profound forgiveness – and relief from my emotional pain.

I now understand that when love touches our pain, we heal. We heal to the extent that we let that love in to touch and transform that part of us that carries the emotional pain. The source of that love within us is the spiritual heart. It is the instrument of love. Love is not only its access code, love is its nature – and therefore, it is your nature and mine.

Chapter 2
What Opened My Heart

That experience of being overwhelmed with the amazing feelings of love healed my pain, brought forgiveness, and opened my awareness to the transformative presence of the spiritual heart. I have shared this first experience of the power of my spiritual heart because it made real for me – and I hope for you – the transformative potential of our spiritual hearts. Years later, I would realize that the experience was possible not only because of my asking, but also because my heart was opened by the access code that lets us connect directly with our spiritual hearts.

As I reflected on that experience, I realized that an event had happened just a moment before I felt that ecstatic love. I now understand that this event opened my heart, so that I could receive the powerful love that so deeply impacted me. In this event I experienced what I have come to realize is the access code to the spiritual heart.

The event happened while I watched Lisa playing on the floor that day. It was just days after her first birthday. I felt warm feelings of love and care for my daughter. However, my emotional pain at that time was so great that the pain numbed much of my feeling of love.

The experience with my baby that evening became different. I had been playing with her on the floor. I got up and sat on the couch while she continued to play on the floor. I saw Lisa reach out for something – and suddenly I realized she wasn't playing with something. She was playing with someone. It was someone I could not see. I saw her reach forward, as she had done so many times toward her mother – then pull back, just as she did when her mother had reached out to touch her. She started to laugh in that beautiful, carefree way of the delighted child who is safe and happy in the embrace of the mother who loved her and provided the safety, love and care that was her entire world. In amazement, I watched them play. By this time, I was sure it was Kathy she was playing with. Her delight was so total, and her movements were ones that were so familiar to me, from many evenings of having watched that wonderful pair at play.

I remembered so often looking over from my desk where I was studying, my attention drawn by the giggles. It might be a toy being passed back and forth, or hugs and tickles, and responses with toes and noses. It was the magic of love in its simplest, deepest, most beautiful form – the exquisite love of a mother for her baby.

As I watched them this night, only able to see one part of this precious exchange, my heart opened. I was so deeply touched. I was so grateful for whatever it was that made it possible for this loving mother to reach from beyond our world into the child's to touch and engage her. My heart filled with pure, beautiful feelings of tenderness, of care, and of love. My pain of loss could not limit these exquisite feelings. I was experiencing again one of the most beautiful moments of our small family's world. Those moments had always filled my heart. Even though I could only see Lisa and her actions, I felt and treasured the love that in that moment was being expressed to this precious child.

It was then, immersed in those feelings of love and gratefulness, that I experienced the overwhelming love for me that I have shared with you. That moment witnessing mother and baby playing together took me into the feelings that are the access code for the spiritual heart. Perhaps it was also knowing that my baby was in her mother's good care that helped me to let go. In the moment that followed, I was filled with love.

It was a love that was so much greater than any feeling I have ever experienced – and yet it was thoroughly personal. It was cosmic and intimate. In that experience, love so filled me that nothing else existed. It did not feel like Kathy's personal love, yet as I reflect back I can't help but feel that a part of her presence with Lisa and with me that evening was the gift of her personal love. And it helped to open the door – that I might receive the full, amazing love that flows through my spiritual heart. This love was so great that it would forever change my life.

Through that direct experience, I was shown in the only way that could ever have had true meaning for me the true power and presence of the love that is present in, as and through our spiritual hearts.

Chapter 3
Heart Connection

How do we connect with our spiritual heart? The primary reason most of us don't know how to connect with our spiritual heart is that we are not designed to connect without the access code. That may seem strange – it always has to me – to have this powerful source of personal attunement within us, and yet not be designed to use it all the time.

Our primary method of interpreting what happens in our lives and selecting our response is not with our hearts. It is with our brains. Our primary perceptual mechanism is in our head. It is through our brains that we gather life's data and interpret it cognitively and emotionally.

What happens when something comes to our awareness? Let's use my experience of an ice cream truck pulling up at a beach as an example I have experienced over the years. The first thing I hear is a happy tune that plays from the truck as it pulls up at the curb. That data, the music, comes into my ear and is distributed across my brain (the cortex) by a part of the brain called the thalamus. My cortex (the thinking part of my brain) will come up with the recognition of the sound. It will recognize the tune – and that this sound means "ice cream truck."

However, even before my cortex gets to the details, the emotional memory processor in my brain – the amygdala – will have already taken the data of that sound and checked it against my emotional memory database. It will connect with a positive emotional memory of ice cream and laughing children. As a result, I will already be feeling good by the time my cortex puts the ice cream truck response into my awareness. Although emotional memory seems to be distributed throughout the body, the processor is in the brain, and it is super fast.

If I experienced a different stimulus, such as spotting a shark fin out in the water – even before I cognitively identified it as a shark fin – my amygdala would have taken the raw data coming in from my eyes, compared it to my emotional memories, and created a fear reaction within me. Even before I could think "Shark fin!" I would have been sitting up straighter and feeling fear.

These two mechanisms from the brain, the cognitive and the emotional, provide me with most of my view of the world around me and what it means to me. These basic functions are always on the job when I am awake.

My heart's role in those moments at the beach was limited to that of the physical heart. It probably would have speeded up a little from a sense of positive excitement upon hearing the ice cream truck. It also would have sped up upon getting the fear signal from the amygdala about the shark fin. The spiritual heart would have remained neutral because it had not been called upon. My brain handles my interpretation of my life experiences, and creates how I react to them.

Scientific research has shown that we have the capability to choose to connect with our hearts in such a way that our hearts change our brains, and bring about a different perception of our life experiences. All people have had that experience, although it is seldom intentional or recognized. Very few people know how to intentionally create that shift of perception. The discovery of how to do this is the greatest spiritual discovery of our time.

This connection to our hearts is accomplished primarily through our feelings. We have the ability to select feelings that activate a connection with our hearts. When that connection is made, we are able to experience a different perception of the events unfolding in that moment. That new perception is the result of our spiritual hearts expressing through the mechanism of our physical hearts.

The impact of this change of perception can be powerful and profound. It changes how we feel and the choices we see before us. We will explore in detail the feelings that are the heart's access code and how to activate them even in times of duress.

Chapter 4
Your Heart's Wisdom

As wonderful as it is to be able to transform our feeling world at will, there is another quality that is an even more powerful and exciting gift of the spiritual heart. It stunned me when I realized I could access this additional unique quality of the spiritual heart. I call it wisdom. This quality, more than anything else I have ever worked with, has brought forth the meaning and positive potential of my life. It has also done so for many other people.

In my search to understand what it is that brings about the kind of transformation that I and many others have experienced, I came across researchers who were looking into human transformation scientifically. I began exploring their research. The people I encountered worked at The HeartMath® Institute, which I'll just call HeartMath®. They talked about the "heart's intelligence." At that time, they were just beginning to publish information about this unique domain of intelligence. I certainly had never heard of it.

My education took place through the 1960s and 1970s in college and law school, as well as through focused spiritual studies. All dealt with intelligence, and never was the heart mentioned as a possible source of my intelligence. I began exploring this amazing idea with a large dose of skepticism.

What I have found from years of exploring this quality of the heart that HeartMath® calls "heart intelligence" has been profound. To me, the best term for this important quality of your spiritual heart is simply wisdom. What I can now tell you from my experience, and from what others have shared with me, is that your heart is wise. It is amazingly wise. Your physical heart is the doorway to a wisdom that is always there to guide you. It is a wisdom that is so powerful that it knows the answers to your every question. It is a wisdom so great that it knows your needs and helps you understand the needs of others. Its wisdom is greater than that of your brain. It is greater than what you have acquired from the schools you have attended and the books you have read.

This wisdom can instruct you. Plus, its power can lift you, heal you and carry you beyond the challenges in your life to a fulfillment beyond your wildest dreams. This wisdom has power to change the world around you, and to change you profoundly. This wisdom is your best friend. This wisdom is really your true self. It is the expression of who you really are at the core of your being. Before you were born into your body, this wisdom was guiding you, choosing a path for you, and setting your true goals upon your heart.

This wisdom is your spiritual heart. This wisdom is the power of your true heart, radiating through the wonderful doorway of your physical heart.

To understand the spiritual heart's wisdom, I had to apply it in my own life. It was by personal experience that I began to realize this huge potential that I have been sharing with you.

My first test of this wisdom came when I was in a professional position that was very uncomfortable. A man was creating a conflict between himself and another leader that would cause a major problem for the organization I was responsible for. I knew that the problem would result in a painful conflict – and hurt feelings for a number of people important to the organization's success – myself included.

I tried for some time to come up with a way of successfully handling this situation to avoid the negative impacts on everyone involved. This was a non-profit organization, and the people involved were volunteers. They all, including this man, cared about the organization. Something in this situation had triggered a level of this man's condemnation toward the leader, which grew with every attempt to defuse it. I could not figure out any way to bring a resolution that would not cause a deep rift, affecting everyone.

One day, I was sitting at my desk, feeling anxious and worried about how to handle this situation. These are feelings I don't like – and yet they seemed unavoidable at that moment.

Suddenly I remembered that I had learned how to stop stress. Well, that was what I was told when I had taken a training during my recent first visit to

HeartMath®. They taught me some steps that they said engaged my heart, and that this had the power to stop the stress I was feeling. Even if I could not avoid or solve the problem, at least I could give myself a break from the stress of the worry and anxiety. Not only was that a worthwhile goal for me, I was also curious to see if the technique worked as they said it would.

I went through the set of steps that were designed to access my heart. In less than two minutes, I had completed the steps and was sitting there quietly. I was no longer feeling any stress. I felt no anxiety and I was not worrying. That was a relief. I actually felt good. That was more than just a relief. That was very, very good!

To accomplish this, I performed a simple set of steps that opened my heart, and its power transformed my feelings. That success was an exciting revelation to me. I had not known that my heart had the power to do that.

However, I had added on some additional steps that I had been told would help me access what they called the intelligence of my heart. It had just taken a short additional time, maybe thirty or forty-five seconds, right after the initial steps. As a result of those additional steps, as I was sitting at my desk, I experienced something I did not think was possible. I had a clear understanding of how to deal with this problem successfully.

I also "knew" that this way of responding to the problem would be effective. Not only was I not feeling stress, worry or anxiety, I now had an effective solution to the problem itself. I had accomplished this in only two minutes, by accessing what I would later discover was my spiritual heart. This solution was given to me by my heart's wisdom. I followed this experience by acting on the direction given – and the problem resolved itself without the anticipated conflict.

At that point, my skepticism about "heart intelligence" began to disappear. Awareness of an effective way of handling a challenging problem in your life is to me the perfect definition of real intelligence. I received that direction not from my head, which had examined the problem many times, but from my heart. When I activated my spiritual heart and asked for guidance, what I received was wisdom that was practical, effective and empowering. Wow! That is a fantastic capability to have available to us – at any time, in any situation.

The people at HeartMath®, where I learned the technique, called the expanded awareness and effective insight "heart intelligence." As I have worked with this response within myself and others, I have come to see it as coming through the physical heart from our spiritual self. To me, it is spiritual wisdom.

These two capacities – transforming your feeling world and accessing your profound wisdom – are available to you through your spiritual heart. What I did in those two minutes, you too can do. It was not hard, but it did take sincere intentional focus to move through those steps effectively. Sometimes I have had to take three minutes, even five or ten minutes. In some of the most difficult times in my life, I have been able to use my heart to transform my feelings – and make clear its wisdom – in less than thirty seconds.

That power and wisdom is within you, and finding it in those moments is so very meaningful. The more I used it, the more I learned aspects of its power and wisdom that I find tremendously exciting. These too I want to share with you, because they have made so much difference in my life. My heart says to me that they could also do that in yours. That would make my heart sing.

Chapter 5
Missing the Bus

It has been in life's daily challenges that I find I have the potential to experience a life of meaning and quality – or the lack of it. As I learned to access my spiritual heart more and more in life's ordinary day-to-day situations, I found the quality of my daily life not just growing, but expanding exponentially.

I had a very simple experience that helped me recognize how powerful and effective my spiritual heart could be in my life's everyday problems.

I was driving my two younger children down the hillside to catch the school bus. It is now many years after Kathy's death. My little baby, Lisa, is now happily married and creating a meaningful life of her own. I have met a wonderful woman, Kathryn, whose love has filled my life and helped me continue in my healing and growing. Kathryn has been a wonderful mother to Lisa, and they have a beautiful bond. We have two delightful children of our own, Peter and Anna, who are now in their early teenage years.

At this point, we were living in California's beautiful Santa Cruz Mountains. We lived in what looked like a cozy little cottage on a hillside, at the foot of giant redwood trees, in one of that range's magnificent redwood forests. The home was lovely and took care of the four of us well. It was almost a picture-postcard setting. The only real downside was that Kathryn and I, with our two teenage children, Peter and Anna, shared a single bathroom. If you have had teenage children, or know of someone who has, you will understand that a single bathroom before school and work in the morning is bound to cause a little, or a lot, of friction and frustration.

It was one of those mornings when everything in the house had been chaotic. The children took too long in the bathroom, couldn't find their homework, and had misplaced their clothes. We were running late. It was a pattern that had happened over and over again. Only this time, "We'll miss the bus!" wasn't a worry. It was a reality.

The bus was gone by the time we drove down the hillside and reached the bus stop. It was a long drive to school. I didn't have time to drive the children to school because I needed to be at work soon. I was frustrated and angry. I had asked and asked the children to start earlier, and not let all these things get left to the last moment, so that this wouldn't happen.

I had been reading a book on parenting that talked about letting children experience the consequences of their actions. In this situation, that probably meant having them walk to school. I wasn't comfortable with that, as the school was over eight miles away. We already knew we could not catch up to the school bus because it took a very different route through the forest. We had tried that before. I could not drive them, and I was upset. There was no good way that I could see to deal with this situation.

As we sat there at the bus stop, I remembered about my spiritual heart. Maybe I needed its help. I did need help with how to deal with getting the kids to school. Plus, I don't like the feeling of being upset even when I "have a right to be." Maybe this was one of those moments to see if my spiritual heart was available when things went wrong.

I took a moment, actually about ninety seconds, to activate my spiritual heart and ask for its help. (I'll share with you, in Chapter 7, the steps I took to do that.) As I went through the steps, I felt my body change. I felt the relief as the emotional tension within me released. I experienced a sudden insight that translated itself into a clear thought, that both felt right and was a relief. The important thing is – it worked. At the end of the ninety seconds, I felt calm. I felt more than calm – I actually felt good.

I not only knew what to do, I was looking forward to it. I understood what was important here, and I knew how to resolve the conflicts around the issues that were so frustrating to me just moments before.

I was now looking at this situation very differently than I had, just ninety seconds before. My perspective changed. I had shifted into connection with personal values that were very important to me, values that were not even in my thoughts ninety seconds earlier.

As a result of activating my spiritual heart, my concern shifted from my needs to my children's needs. I was aware that they had experienced a very stressful morning. All the chaos – the pressure to find the missing homework, and the race down the mountain, and now being late for the bus – was stressful for *them*. I realized we all played a part in being late – myself included.

They were concerned about getting to school late. They knew that I was upset over missing the bus, and both of these things put pressure on them. Just as I had a full and demanding day before me, so did they. For teenagers, school holds many demands and stresses that are very significant in their world.

I was the one who could get to work late. My co-workers would understand. We were all adults, and many of them also had children.

I turned to my children and said, "I'll drive you to school today. I want you to be relaxed and have a good day. Will you work with me tomorrow so that this doesn't happen again?" They both looked very relieved, and promised me they would. I put on some relaxing music and started the long drive to the school.

I felt good. I felt peaceful. I was glad to be caring for my children, and helping them out of a difficult situation. I felt our closeness as a family. In addition, I was at peace being late for my work. I am a very punctual person who is consistently on time. A little flexibility is a good thing.

My spiritual heart responded to my invitation by changing my perception. It put me in touch with my feelings of care for my children. It activated my intuition, which enabled me to understand their needs. It released me from my attitude of blaming, and my judgments about who should have done what, when. My spiritual heart brought my feeling world from frustration and anxiety to clarity and peace. It guided me on how to handle my time conflict in releasing my judgmental response, and replacing it with acceptance and flexibility. From that point forward, I had a lovely day.

When our spiritual nature directs our experiences of life, those experiences change. We are suddenly experiencing what is taking place in our lives differently. I want to say the experience becomes dimensionally different, because I find it difficult to adequately express the magnitude of that difference.

The response I experienced at the bus stop did not feel like just a good idea. That response felt to me dimensionally different from what I was experiencing just a few minutes earlier.

Do you remember when you discovered that you loved someone? Do you remember how magnificent they became in your eyes? How beautiful, how wise, how strong, or how gracious?

That was a gift from your spiritual heart. You began to see them with your spiritual eyes. You understood that person from a deeper place of wisdom within yourself. You activated your spiritual heart – and you touched, and were touched by, their spirit.

Your physical heart is the doorway through which your spiritual self enters into your life experience of the moment. Another of the gifts that results from your spiritual heart, working with and through your physical heart, is the often-elusive experience we refer to as peace.

When we were late for the bus, I was tense. I was frustrated. I was angry and blaming my children. Ninety seconds later I was at peace and I knew what to do. Wow! To be able to connect with a power that transforms me like that is a real treasure.

Chapter 6
Accessing Wisdom

My favorite gift of the spiritual heart is wisdom. I have so often been in a situation where I believed that there was no good answer. I have been so convinced that nothing could be done that I almost didn't call upon my spiritual heart. Fortunately, sometimes I did it anyway. I would take the steps because I had made a commitment to myself to ask my heart. After all, what is one or two or even five minutes?

I would go through the steps, and suddenly I would be aware of an answer. I was aware of how to deal with the situation. I was seeing the situation differently, and I knew how to go forward successfully.

It is one of the most beautiful moments in life when we discover the amazing wisdom responding to us through our spiritual hearts. I have often laughed at myself when this wisdom's response came to my awareness. It has seemed as if what my heart just told me to do should have been obvious (like putting on the relaxing music and driving my children to school in a supporting, nurturing way when we missed the bus).

However, that wasn't a choice that my mind came up with. My attention and actions before I engaged my heart were directed by the emotions of frustration that were running through my system at the time.

Having told you of my children's commitment to address our lateness in the mornings, I can't help but share what I observed from my daughter Anna. Anna, who at this time was twelve or thirteen, is a year and a half younger than her brother Peter. Peter had developed that "older brother ability" to come up with the thing to do or say, or the look that seemed so innocent, that would instantly upset Anna and set off an intense emotional reaction. One of those regular situations was about using the only bathroom in the house in the morning before school.

Anna had complained to me about Peter taking so much time in the bathroom in the morning, which she knew he was "doing on purpose." She had learned how to access her spiritual heart, so I reminded her of those steps and suggested she try it. (I'll go over the steps in the next chapter.)

The next day we had no trouble getting to the bus on time. I also noticed a smile on Anna's face. That evening I checked with her on what had happened.

She reported that she was about to start shouting at Peter to get out of the bathroom that morning, when she remembered to check with her heart. She went through the steps she had learned. Several things happened. She realized that her shouting was just what Peter wanted, and it would make him take longer if he knew it upset her. She understood she would get in faster if she stayed very quiet, so that he did not know she was outside waiting. She also felt different. Instead of mad and frustrated, she felt smart – and she felt she was getting the better of the situation.

She stepped back into the bedroom closest to the bathroom and waited quietly. She did not make any noise. Peter came out of the bathroom, and the minute he turned to go down the stairs, she jumped into the bathroom. She got in much quicker than usual. Her smile let me know that she felt very good about this new approach. I enjoyed her success – and the lack of pressure in getting out the door to start our ride to the bus.

Sometimes our spiritual heart's wisdom seems like the natural result of the shift out of our emotional turmoil. In the situation where the man was creating a conflict between himself and another leader of the organization, I had thought about that situation and my alternatives many times. Some of these times, I probably felt angry or frustrated. At other times, however, I was peaceful. Yet my brain did not come up with the answer, even in that peaceful state. The answer I needed did not surface to my awareness until I activated my spiritual heart and called upon its wisdom.

What is it that you really want to know? What is it that has seemed to elude you? Within you is a much deeper, more powerful and effective wisdom than that which you have normally accessed – even in your best moments of intellectual brilliance. That is the wisdom of your spiritual heart.

As you meet your life's challenges, big and little, you have this same opportunity to take the steps that activate your spiritual heart and call upon its wisdom.

As you experience its wisdom, I know that you too can find a whole new level of effectiveness and satisfaction from your spiritual heart.

Chapter 7
The Heart Wisdom Tool*

We have touched on many of the gifts that come from activating our spiritual hearts. Now, let's address the "how" question. How can you make these changes take place for you? What are the steps that activate your spiritual heart?

Accessing your spiritual heart is amazingly simple. It begins even before that first step, with the action that is at the core of all transformation modalities – the step of self-awareness. It begins with recognizing "I'm stressed, I'm upset, I'm frustrated, or I'm angry." It is recognizing that whatever is happening has taken us to a place that doesn't feel good. That moment of self-awareness begins our transformation.

---

* The Heart Wisdom Tool is based upon and is a modification of the technique called Freeze-Frame®, used and modified with the permission of The HeartMath® Institute. They have allowed me to present this modified version because of my understanding of the heart and our many years of close association.

Self-awareness is the doorway we step through so that we can take our first step.

Here are the steps to access your spiritual heart. I call these steps The Heart Wisdom Tool.

The Heart Wisdom Tool Step 1: Touch & Breathe

Begin by simply touching your heart with your hand.

This simple gesture becomes the habit that pulls you into a state where you are receptive to connection with your heart. Whenever you feel tense, the simple action of touching your hand to your heart creates a heart connection. It is this connection that invites you to activate your spiritual heart.

The next action is really part of the first step. As you place your hand on your heart, breathe for a moment though your heart. (You and I both know you can't really breathe through your heart – that happens through our lungs and nose. However, you can pretend to breathe through your heart!) Pretending to breathe through the area around your heart focuses your attention on the presence of the transformative power in your heart.

Take a long, deep breath through your heart.

Step 1: Touch & Breathe is quite simple. As you practice it regularly, it becomes your natural response to any stimulation where you begin to feel uncomfortable or overwhelmed. Touch your hand to your heart and breathe through your heart – Touch & Breathe.

The Heart Wisdom Tool Step 2: Remember & Feel

The second step is the one that activates the transformation within your heart. It is the power step. It is where you take hold of the activation code for the spiritual heart.

The activation code is a heart feeling – the experience of a feeling that is connected to the greater feeling of love. Instead of trying to use our heads to define and identify feelings that might be connected to the feeling of love, use the heart itself to guide you to those feelings.

You can enter into a heart feeling by remembering a moment when your heart was full. You might remember a moment when you felt deep appreciation for someone who is special to you. Remember how your heart seemed to swell with that feeling. It is a wonderful feeling. It is positive, uplifting, warm and powerful. That feeling, that powerful feeling of appreciation or deep care, is a heart feeling. It is the access code to your spiritual heart.

Perhaps you remember a delightful moment of watching the sunlight dancing off the water, as dolphins jumped and twisted in the air – your heart felt so wonderfully full. This is the step into your deep heart feelings – the feelings contained within that magnificent memory.

I often go to memories of heart-filled moments that repeat themselves frequently in my life. Our daughter Anna is now grown. Anna, her husband Chris, and their little girl Kirra live in our home with Kathryn and me. Sometimes my memory is just the joyful feeling that fills my heart as I hear little four-year-old Kirra singing, laughing or skipping through the house. Sometimes it is the memory of that delightful moment when Kirra crawls up into my lap as I sit in my big "papa chair," so that we can read a story together.

One of the most powerful of those heart-filled moments for me is the memory of the love I see in Anna's eyes as she looks at little Kirra – so much love. What a wonderful thing to behold – the strong, pure, unconditional, limitless love of this mother for her child. When I remember seeing that look of love upon her face, my heart feels full to overflowing.

Your memory might be the feeling ignited in your heart by the eyes of your life partner as he or she looked adoringly into yours. Your memories might be of moments at weddings that were filled with your happiness for yourself, or for those you love. There might be memories of delightful moments when you recall your carefree laughter with friends. They are all moments when your heart felt full.

Select one of your memories. Remember how you felt in that moment. Feel that wonderful feeling that filled that moment. Experience the feeling. The memory was long ago. The feeling you are experiencing is right now. It is here in you. It is powerful. Remember and feel.

Remember that moment of your hands holding the rope, and swinging out over the water, as you let go – splashing down into the sudden, wet chill and exhilaration of the lake. Remember a moment of joy while playing with friends as a child, maybe dashing away in a game of tag, perhaps clapping and chanting a rhyme together or releasing that freezing snowball as you ducked down to escape one coming your way. Remember the cold touch of the drops of water from the sprinkler as you ran through its wet splash – so inviting and exciting on a hot summer day. Remember the exquisite, tender fullness in your heart while holding a young child in your arms as it drifted off to sleep. Remember and feel. Enjoy those wonderful heart feelings.

"Remember & Feel" is our second step. When you do the second step, you are transformed. You are changed. Your physical heart has opened, and it has let the power of your spiritual heart in. There is no longer the feeling of overwhelm. There is no longer the frustration. Your physical heart has transformed your body, and your spiritual heart's power frees you from the emotional reactions that a moment ago limited and debilitated your life. You are now free of your brain's need to make you fight or run away. You now have access to the centeredness, the calm or the passion that this moment or situation is really about for you.

Two simple steps – Touch & Breathe, and then Remember & Feel – and you are free. That is always a "Wow" for me. You are free of the emotional angst or discomfort. You are free of the way your mind was processing your world. Your spiritual heart's power flows through your system, and its wisdom is within reach.

The Heart Wisdom Tool Step 3: Sincere Asking

We have talked about the next amazing piece of the potential that your spiritual heart holds for you. This is the step where your heart gives you the new perspective. This is where your heart gives you its wisdom. You receive the amazing wisdom to understand: to understand yourself, to understand another person, to understand the situation wisely.

This calling forth of your spiritual heart's wisdom, how does that get activated? How do you call it into awareness?

Like our other steps, this one is simple. Our spiritual heart's wisdom is activated simply by sincerely asking.

"Sincere Asking" is our third and final step. With steps 1 and 2 you can stop the stress. You can become resilient in your emotional and feeling worlds; however, there is a key to your world of wisdom. It is an important key. It is the experience of deep sincerity.

Sincerity is the tool that calls this inner wisdom from your soul – from your spiritual self – into clear, conscious awareness. Sincere asking has the power to fill you with the insight that lets you express the highest that you are.

Sincerity powers your heart's response. Sincerity calls your wisdom forward to be translated into thought by your brain, a brain that is now in service to the heart. Your heart's sincerity is the power that calls forth the wisdom of your soul.

What do you ask? This is a legitimate question. Anyone who has explored life's challenges knows that our questions themselves make a difference. What do you ask?

The question that keeps calling forth the best response for me is the question I was first given when I was learning how to access my heart's wisdom by the people at HeartMath®. The question they suggested was very simple, and it has proven for me to be the best one I have found. It is the question, "What is a more effective response to this situation?" I found that if I asked this question, my heart responded and let me know what I needed to know. It made clear to me how I needed to respond to what was taking place. When I did not know what to do about the man who was creating a conflict that would disrupt my organization, I asked, "What is a more effective response to this situation?" That worked for me in that moment. I was able to receive my heart's simple, profound wisdom.

When I was at the bus stop without a workable alternative, I asked my heart, "What is a more effective response to this situation?" In response to my asking, I suddenly saw the situation differently. My spiritual heart told me how to take care of my children, and it brought to my awareness how I could address my own need as well.

This is my question. What is your question? I am discovering that we each have the ability to discover the question that brings resolution to the conflicts before us. Our heart has the question – and the answers – already available for us. I find that the simple question, "What do you want me to know?" helps some people connect with their spiritual hearts.

Sometimes, the need for action is so great that the question for our hearts is "What do you want me to do?" Sometimes, when the situation seems too big or complex, I find it helpful to ask "What is an effective next step?"

My suggestion is that you start with my question, "What is a more effective response to this situation?" While you practice and learn the steps, this is an excellent question to work with. It is easier, after you have worked with this for a time, to then find if there is another question that works well for you.

Although the question is important, what makes the greatest difference is something else entirely. What makes the greatest difference in the power, and the receptiveness we have to our answers, is our sincerity.

Sincerity is the powerful heart feeling that draws wisdom from the soul into our awareness. Sincerity is the power that draws the spiritual self into active engagement in our lives.

Think back on the questions you have asked in your life. Do you remember any questions like "Why did this happen to me?" and others that may have been passionately spoken, but were really said from frustration, anger, impatience, judgment or that magnificent of motivators, the feeling of "poor me"?

Sincerity is different. Sincerity is that heart desire to understand. Sincerity doesn't care if I am right or wrong, or if I have to leave or stay. Sincerity comes from the deep desire within our hearts to show up as who we really are. It comes from our deep desire to help – and to make a difference, a wise difference. It is there to take us forward, to draw us into an engagement in life that holds meaning and purpose for us.

Sincerely ask your heart, "What is a more effective response?"

I'm sure that there have been times in your life when it was no longer important to get the answer you wanted. You sincerely desired to really know how to respond effectively to whatever was before you. I know you have reached that place at times; we all have. There was no more win, or lose, or self-justification. It was powerful then, and you will find that each time you enter that place of sincerity, you will feel its power now.

The Heart Wisdom Tool
1. Touch & Breathe
   a. Touch your heart, & breathe slow, deep breaths through your heart.
2. Remember & Feel
   a. Remember a time when your heart was full.
3. Sincere Asking
   a. What is a more effective response?

These steps are amazingly simple for being so powerful. Imagine yourself in a situation where you are feeling stress, pressure or worry. You naturally find yourself taking that first step, Touch & Breathe. You place your hand on your heart, and pretend to take several long deep breaths through your heart. It is so natural, and so easy.

As your attention shifts to the area of your heart, your breathing invites you to focus on the second step of "Remember & Feel." This is when you remember that moment when your heart felt full.

My memory often goes to a time when Kathryn and I were in Hawaii, out whale watching in a little raft. It was a beautiful day, with the deep blue of the water capped by huge, puffy, white cumulus clouds that majestically filled the sky. I was enjoying the feeling of the light caress of the boat's spray, when suddenly humpback whales we had glimpsed in the distance turned and began to swim toward our raft. The raft stopped still in the water, and our gazes were riveted on the dark bodies as they broke the surface of the water, blowing their breath as a dynamic white mist into the air – catching and sparkling in the sunlight – signaling that they were drawing closer to our small craft. Even though each one was many times bigger than our raft I felt no fear. My heart was filled with an excited sense of wonder. The whales dove a short distance away from us, their tails breaking the surface and then disappearing. We watched, enthralled, as their massive bodies passed directly under our small raft. The sun illuminated their bodies through the water. They were huge, blue, white and dark gray, mystical and magnificent. Then they surfaced on the other side of our little raft – and my heart was filled with overflowing joy at seeing the beauty, the majesty and the magnificence of these creatures. I can still feel the radiant fullness of my heart, overflowing with joy, delight and wonder. I can still feel it.

Take hold of your memory. As its images surface in your awareness, open to the feeling that was in your heart. Experience again the powerful feeling from your heart-filled memory. Your heart can still feel the fullness, remembering and feeling. When you have enjoyed that feeling, luxuriating as it impacts every cell of your body, then go to that place of deep sincerity.

Imagine yourself taking that third step, Sincere Asking. Ask from the sincerity of your heart, "What is a more effective response?" With your sincerity, your mind is receptive as your heart sends its clear wisdom into your awareness through your thoughts. There is a beautiful peace in your heart as you understand the next steps before you.

You took the steps.
1. Touch & Breathe
2. Remember & Feel
3. Sincere Asking

Now you are transformed and guided by your spiritual heart.

Chapter 8
Intuitive Wisdom

Your spiritual heart is intuitive. That is one of the reasons why the response of your spiritual heart is so insightful.

The two-and-a-half watts of electrical energy generated by your beating heart creates an electromagnetic field. Some scientists have called that heart-generated field the intuitive field. As the physical heart changes and is impacted by the spiritual heart, it enhances our intuitive capacity.

At the school bus stop, the change I made by activating my spiritual heart opened my intuitive connection with my children. In that moment I intuitively understood their stress, their frustrations and their needs. When my head, with its frustration, was creating the world I saw, that intuitive connection was shut down. That intuitive field was closed.

When Anna connected with her spiritual heart, she understood her brother and what would make a difference in her situation. Her heart's wisdom used that intuitive insight to direct her into a path of action that was effective for her.

I'm sure you have been in that same situation, with someone you cared about, where you suddenly had an intuitive insight. You "knew" or had an understanding into their situation, and saw a way to be of help. That is the intuitive capacity we access most easily and directly though our spiritual hearts.

The scientists are able to explain the biophysical and electromagnetic changes that result in the opening of this intuitive capacity. With it, we sense and understand the needs of those around us at a deeper level. My children in our car, when we missed the bus, had needs and experiences that I sensed and understood when my heart opened, giving me access to my intuition.

I have noticed that I perceive the world differently when I am in my spiritual heart. I am aware of what is taking place around me at a different level. This intuitive capacity of the spiritual heart will result in your perceiving your situations as a whole. You will find that you understand the situation with sensitivity to other's roles and needs, as well as your own. Your new understanding will include expanded feelings and thoughts, as well as expanded awareness. The spiritual heart's wisdom can direct you to an effective interaction with this greater whole that you now perceive.

The importance of this amazing intuitive capacity of your heart is hard to overestimate. For most of us, the vast majority of our challenges involve other people.

Have you found yourself in situations that were becoming difficult because you didn't know what the other person was thinking or feeling? The way they were responding made no sense to you? Without your intuition, you were left out of important information that was influencing your world. In those kinds of situations, I have found that when my spiritual heart was activated, I gained some understanding of the other person. Suddenly I was able to glimpse into their thoughts, needs and feelings.

I went from feeling separate or isolated from that person to finding myself understanding, or at least having a sense of how to respond to them. I found a sense of connection with them, thanks to the intuitive capacity of my spiritual heart. As a result, my heart directive was more effective for us both. Your spiritual heart also has that capability. By activating it, that intuitive wisdom becomes yours too.

One of the great gifts in my life has been that others have shared with me their experiences of connecting with their hearts. Some of these have been a simple understanding of how to deal effectively with a life challenge or question. Other insights have been more startling, because those insights resulted in the heart-resolving issues that the head had been dealing with for years. Their spiritual hearts revealed a completely different insight or understanding of themselves, and of another person, from what the mind had been holding.

When I have presented workshops on how to access one's heart, after people have received an answer from their heart, I have occasionally asked how many of them found responses that they had never considered before. There are consistently 10 to 20 percent who find a totally new perspective. The other 80 to 90 percent had previously experienced the insight as a thought or idea, but had discounted or totally rejected it.

This is quite understandable, since the heart is suggesting wise approaches to us throughout our lives. If our spiritual heart is not activated, we do not have the deeper understanding to realize the importance of the thought that carries the heart's wisdom. Because of the way the brain processes and explores alternatives, we are seldom able to recognize the true wisdom and effectiveness of the heart's suggestions.

People often describe that experience by saying that the heart's wisdom, which is so clear to them after they intentionally engage their spiritual heart, was just a random thought before. They did not understand its value, prior to activating their spiritual hearts.

When a person has never even thought of what the heart reveals, they receive the wonderful awareness that what seemed hopeless is hopeless no longer.

What a freeing gift this is – a gift from the intuitive capacity of their spiritual heart!

A woman once shared with me that she had tried activating her spiritual heart, calling on its wisdom in a situation that she believed to be hopeless. She was deeply frustrated by her relationship with her sister. The two had been estranged for more than a dozen years. The woman thought about it often, and tried everything she could think of to open a positive relationship with her sister, whom she really cared about.

The woman was learning about her spiritual heart in a workshop I was leading. She decided to see if it would help in this hopeless situation. She activated her spiritual heart. What did she have to lose? She called on its wisdom. She focused on her steps for ninety seconds – maybe it was even two minutes. Then I saw her smile. She wrote something on a sheet of paper, and then kept writing. She was radiant. She turned to her husband, who was seated beside her, and began sharing excitedly with him.

A few minutes later, I asked the people in the room if anyone wanted to share what had happened for them. She joyously shared that she had been estranged from her sister for many years, and had tried everything to reconnect, to no avail. Now, she knew what to do and how to do it. She said she *knew* it would work. Her smile was radiant.

It is one of the most beautiful moments in life when we discover the amazing wisdom responding to us through our spiritual hearts. That wisdom is there for you.

1. Touch & Breathe
2. Remember & Feel
3. Sincere Asking

Chapter 9
Accessing Our Values

I have so often found myself deeply grateful for what is to me the wisdom of my spiritual heart. This quality guides me at a level that continues to amaze me. It can also do that for you.

I shared with you the wisdom around my experience of missing the school bus, and the woman's guidance on how to reconnect with her sister. When I examine these experiences, they each appear to be directly connected to our true values. This actually makes sense to me when I think about it. The values that are the most meaningful to us are things that are deeply felt within our hearts. I value responding to others with care. I love my children, and every member of my family. I deeply desire their happiness and well-being. These are qualities I associate with my heart, rather than my head. I may think about them, but mostly they are deep feelings that I have, which seem to go to my core sense of identity. It makes sense that I connect to those values when my spiritual heart is activated.

I have heard thousands of experiences shared with me by people learning to use this powerful aspect of their beings. As I explore with them their heart's direction, it becomes clear that the spiritual heart brings into conscious choice a response to our life situations that is consistent with our deeply held values.

One of the times I experienced this connection most clearly was during a period of major change in my life. Kathryn and I, with Peter and Anna, had just moved from our home in Spokane, Washington, to the Santa Cruz Mountains in California. We were going to work at HeartMath®. This was a very new experience for us – a major career change for both Kathryn and me, as well as a whole new world for the children. We had also just celebrated Lisa's wedding to a wonderful young man. It had been a beautiful experience. We were so happy for her. Our hearts were full and our expectations were high.

We were getting settled in our new home when Kathryn expressed concern over a physical condition. She saw a doctor, who arranged an outpatient surgery to take care of the problem.

I took her in for the surgery, and waited in the outpatient clinic's waiting room. After more than an hour, the doctor came out dressed in his surgical garb and motioned for me to join him in the hall. I remember that he had on one of those formless green tunics, paper booties on his feet, and a head covering over his hair. The mask that covers his nose and mouth in surgery was around his neck. There, in the hallway, which was narrow but at least out of earshot of anyone in the waiting room, he updated me on the situation with Kathryn. He told me that he stopped her surgical procedure because he had "discovered a situation that could be life threatening." He said that she would need to be hospitalized for major surgery.

As he spoke these words, I felt an immediate sense of panic and fear. My body tensed, and my mind immediately focused on two very different aspects of what he said.

71

First, we were there without medical insurance. The idea of hospitalization for major surgery was financially far beyond our means. We could barely afford the outpatient procedure that Kathryn was there for. Yet obviously for her well-being – for her life – she needed this surgery to happen. The costs we would face suddenly seemed like an overwhelming obstacle.

My second strong reaction was to his words "life threatening." I had been through my first wife Kathy's death, which I shared with you in the opening chapter. The hurt, loss and pain from that time were triggered in me by the thought that this wonderful woman whom I loved so much might also be facing death.

Those feelings from that earlier time were like a heavy black weight that seemed to pull me down. I thought of the joy, the hope of this exquisitely wise, loving woman that Kathryn is, suddenly looking at life ending before even half her dreams could be born. I saw only the briefest glimpse of the pain that our family would feel if we lost Kathryn, who was the very center of our lives together.

I was paralyzed by these overwhelming feelings – the financial fear, and the fear of death. Both were impossible situations that I seemed to be viewing through a fog, with no idea how to respond. Our hopes and dreams seemed to have suddenly crashed into financial devastation, and ever so much worse than that – Kathryn facing death.

I realized that this was a moment when I needed the help of my spiritual heart. While standing there in the hall with my eyes wide open, listening to the doctor, I activated my spiritual heart.

I went through each of the steps, sincerely engaging and focusing on each one. Having touched my heart and focused on breathing through my heart, I brought to my memory our wonderful experience in Hawaii with the whales. I could hear and receive every word that the doctor spoke to me, and yet I was able to feel again the thrill to my heart as that baby whale leaped into the air. In the final step, I sincerely called upon my spiritual heart's wisdom. "What is a more effective response?"

A moment later, my fears vanished. I felt centered and poised. Most importantly, I knew what I needed to do. When I activated my spiritual heart, it responded immediately by first addressing the two fears that the doctor's statement had awakened within me.

My spiritual heart first brought to my awareness the understanding that there was nothing I could do, standing there in that hall, about the financial needs that the surgery represented. With that realization, I felt the shift of emotion away from my financial panic into a sense of acceptance that this could be addressed at a later time.

The second directive from my spiritual heart was that this situation was not about the death of my first wife. Due to the power of this illumination, I realized that this medical need had nothing to do with that earlier loss, and that I needed to let go of that concern so that I could be fully present to this situation. Even as that thought occurred, I felt the tension and anxious focus from Kathy's death fade away. The feelings of darkness disappeared, and I was free to focus on what my heart really knew was important. What was important for me – deeply important in that moment – was to care for Kathryn.

This connection with my spiritual heart, and its response to my thoughts and my emotional world, took less than a minute. When the doctor finished speaking – I never missed a word he said – I was prepared, and I was able to express to him what was important for me at that moment.

The first responses from my spiritual heart were understandings that addressed my financial and death fears, and then moved me into a calmer, focused state. I also felt my spiritual heart's impact on my body, releasing its tension – as well as clarity returning to my thoughts, and balance to my emotions. I was then able to receive from my heart the further understanding that Kathryn would be frightened, and would need my support. I realized that she would have been conscious, and that the doctor would have informed her of the problem and his decision. She would naturally be feeling vulnerable and afraid.

I said to the doctor that I needed to go and see my wife right away, because she would need my presence and reassurance. He immediately responded, and took me in to see her. I was able to be with her and share my strength with her. I was able to let her know –

because I knew it in my heart – that we would get through this, and she would be healthy and well again.

This focused support for Kathryn with strength instead of fear was what was important, and of real value to me, in that moment. Understanding that importance – its crystal-clear realization – was the gift of my spiritual heart. That realization was an expression of values that I hold. Our spiritual hearts respond to our core values as they uplift and guide us.

My experience at that moment in the hallway with the doctor changed from worries of my mind to the values of my heart. All that my heart had assured us did happen. Kathryn is healthy and well – and we found a way to handle the expenses involved.

That change from worries to values isn't a physical change. The physical changes in my heart did help. The physical changes altered my system so that I could connect with my spiritual heart. I felt my body release its tension. I felt my mind clear. However, the profound change that I experienced wasn't physical. That deep, profound change in my perception, feeling and understanding was the result of the power and wisdom of my spiritual nature that I experienced through my spiritual heart. Its wisdom, its connectedness with me and with my values, was what impacted me – and through me, the situation and my wife.

Those changes were ones that expressed who I really am – not the young man overwhelmed by circumstances – rather, a wise man who is in touch with the real values of his being – and who expresses them.

This wonderful quality, the ability of our spiritual hearts to connect us with the highest aspects or values of our beings, is another of its great gifts. That is important to me. One of my personal values is to show up in life expressing my personal values. Not someone else's values – mine. My spiritual heart makes that possible.

Chapter 10
The Bridge

I was running late one morning. I'm noticing that this isn't the first "I'm late" story. Perhaps that is something I need to pay attention to. Oh well, it's true. I was late.

It was one of those mornings when things just seemed to run behind schedule for both Kathryn and me. We left for work at the same time and often rode together. However, today we were headed in different directions after work, so we were each driving. My car was in the lead as we hurried down the one-lane roads between our home on the redwood-covered mountainside and the main road, which was a two-lane highway. We drove quickly, but still carefully, through the twisty lane that weaved through the majestic redwood trees. My car was in front, so I was the first to reach the one-lane bridge that spanned the creek separating the area of homes from the road. I entered the fairly long bridge, and was about halfway across, when I saw a Volkswagen "Bug" approach the end of the bridge, having come from the highway. The Volkswagen came to the bridge and stopped in front of it.

This surprised me, because there was a pullover area at that end of the bridge so that cars could wait, giving plenty of clearance for the vehicles already on the bridge to exit. Instead of entering the pullover area, the Volkswagen drove right to the end of the bridge and stopped. I was almost across the bridge, so I slowed and stopped because the Volkswagen was blocking my exit. It was directly in my way.

I stopped and waited for it to back up and pull into the pull-over area. It didn't. I waited some more, sure that the person had not been paying attention, and assumed that upon seeing that we had crossed the bridge, they would pull over so we could exit. They didn't.

I looked at my watch, noting that I was late, and yet determined to be patient with this driver. After all, it was sure to dawn on him or her that it was necessary for the car to get out of the way for us. Only then could the Volkswagen enter the bridge, and proceed across. It didn't.

My intention of patience was growing thin. This was an obvious situation. The car on the bridge had the right of way. I had been an attorney at another point in my life; however, I realized that this was not a difficult legal question. It was just common sense. We could not exit the bridge until the car moved out of the way. It didn't.

Now my patience had given way to irritation and frustration. I needed to get to work. I couldn't get off the bridge until the car got out of the way. I needed to go forward, but the Volkswagen was completely blocking the way. It was not possible to get around it. I waited again. Surely the driver would pull over. It just made sense. The driver could see that he or she couldn't get on the bridge until our two cars were off the bridge. Our cars sat there waiting for the Volkswagen to move. It didn't.

Now I realized I was going to have to get out of my car, go up to the Volkswagen, and ask the driver to do what was obvious – to pull over so that we could exit the bridge. I couldn't imagine the driver not knowing that, but if he or she didn't respond, I would have to ask them to pull over. I finally reached for the door handle to get out of the car.

Then I remembered my spiritual heart. It only took ninety seconds to activate my heart. That was time I seemed to have, since I was just sitting there. I decided to activate my spiritual heart. I touched my heart, and took the deep breaths though my heart, as I focused on that area of my body. Then I went to a memory. As I recalled the memory, I enjoyed the feeling. The memory was of how much I loved the feeling of walking through the redwood trees. There were redwood trees on either side of the creek, so the memory was easy to get to.

I had hiked through the redwoods the other day, and I remembered how my heart felt so full as I watched the sunlight dance through the redwood branches. It was a wonderful feeling. I enjoyed the feeling and relaxed into it, letting it completely fill me.

Then I asked. I sincerely asked, "What is a more effective response to this situation?" I didn't really expect an answer. I knew what I had to do. I had to get the car that was blocking the exit to get out of the way. But I asked anyhow, out of habit. My asking was very sincere. I really wanted to know, and I hoped that there was an easier way than getting out and confronting the driver. I knew there wasn't, but I asked anyway, and I asked sincerely.

Suddenly, a clear, directive thought filled my mind. It said, "Back up." That surprised me. Why would I back up? I had a car behind me. I had come all the way across the bridge. I had the right of way. Why would I back up? I asked again, "What is a more efficient response to this situation?" The response this time was the same. "Back up."

I almost laughed this time. My whole view of the situation changed in that moment. I realized that the car behind me was Kathryn, and if I motioned for her to back up, she would. In a moment, we could both be clear of the bridge, and the other car could cross. It would take less time for me to do this than to get out and walk over to the Volkswagen. Plus, I would not have to argue with someone who, it seemed, had some kind of problem.

So I did it. I turned around and motioned for Kathryn to back up. She put her car in reverse, and in a moment had she backed off the bridge and pulled into the turn-out area on the other end of the bridge. A moment later, I did the same thing.

The old Volkswagen drove forward across the bridge and continued on up the road. I pulled onto the bridge, drove across it, and pulled onto the main road, continuing on to work. The effort to clear the bridge and let the Volkswagen go across took about two minutes. That was much less time than if I had gotten out of my car and started a conversation to try to get the other driver to do what he or she was obligated to do.

Time-wise, this was much more effective. I was off to work, which was what was important to me. I didn't need to straighten out the other driver's mind, problem or whatever. I just needed to get to work soon.

The surprising thing about that experience was that I felt fine about clearing the bridge for the car. I wasn't angry or upset. A moment before I activated my spiritual heart, I had a fleeting thought of just driving forward and pushing the smaller Volkswagen out of the way – even though it might have damaged my car. My frustration had been growing in intensity, and moving toward anger, at the unreasonable obstruction blocking my path.

My mind was focused on my being "right." It was focused on going forward. It was focused on getting the other car out of the way.

I had earlier experienced a brief thought of backing up – but I immediately dismissed it. There was a car behind me blocking my way, and "I was in the right!"

My heart changed all of that. It transformed my feelings from anger and frustration to calm efficiency. I was glad to do what took the least time. I was glad to avoid a potentially unpleasant conversation. I was glad to just get going. I did not have any investment in being right, or "winning." I was calm, and grateful for the quick and easy solution.

This is such a simple situation. For me, it served as a moment of recognition of how different my spiritual heart's wisdom is from my head's. It was a moment when I experienced my justifiable negative feelings being transformed – so I was not feeling negative, but instead, peaceful.

I felt better because of my spiritual heart. I thought more clearly because of my spiritual heart. I responded to my true goal and values because of my spiritual heart. And I continued to enjoy my drive through the beautiful redwoods that lined the highway on my way to work because of my spiritual heart. It was the start of a beautiful day.

Chapter 11
Research

I am so grateful that there has been excellent research done on this transformative power of our hearts. I love research. I find that I have a deeply suspicious streak in my nature. Many people have claimed that something was true because they wanted it to be true. Often, when I looked into their assertions, their claims turned out to be mere wishful thinking. I like to see if the data is there to support what they claim. If we are really engaging something of this magnitude, shouldn't we be able to measure its effect on our body and emotions?

Fortunately, I came across the exciting work of HeartMath®. I had asked my heart to guide me to a greater level of personal skill in my spirituality and a greater way to help others. The result was that I found myself exploring this avenue of research.

I actually thought at that time that I knew all about the heart, and about love. Surprise – I didn't. I found that I actually did not know much about it at all.

I got to work extensively with HeartMath's research. I saw how, when the heart feelings we have in our memories are activated, we are freed of physical and emotional reactions created by the brain. We are changed. I felt it physically and emotionally when I did their exercise, but it meant a great deal to me to also see it on the computer screen.

More specifically, there is a change in the heart, which their researchers are able to identify, that shows one of the profound impacts of our spiritual hearts. This measurable change is a change from a disordered pattern of the heart's speeding up and slowing down into an ordered pattern called coherence.

The heart's speeding up and slowing down is called heart rate variability (HRV). It is examined by graphing the heart rate over time. When we are in a state of frustration, the heart rate variability graph (HRV) is highly disordered. There is no pattern to it. The scientists call that an incoherent pattern. When a person shifts from a feeling of frustration to a sincere heart feeling such as appreciation, or a heart-filled memory, this pattern becomes ordered or coherent.

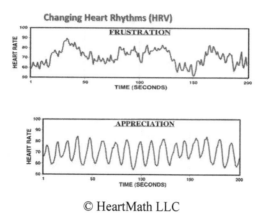

© HeartMath LLC

This is not a minor change. The speeding up and slowing down of the heart is literally transformed from disorder to order, from incoherence to coherence.

This change in the heart's HRV pattern physically changes the parts of the brain we reviewed earlier — the amygdala and the thalamus. This is important because the thalamus impacts the cognitive patterns of our brain, and the amygdala impacts our emotional responses. We think and feel better when our heart is in its coherent state.

What causes this shift? What created the coherent state in the heart? Feeling your heart feelings. That powerful experience when you remember – and feel again the feelings of the moment – when your heart was full. Those feelings cause your heart to change. Your heart then causes your brain to change, up-leveling your emotions and your thinking.

Those feelings transform your heart, which transforms your brain, which transforms your emotions. They don't just improve them a little bit. Their impact is to transform each of these crucial elements of our perceptual nature to an entirely different level of operation.

This discovery that tells us how we can, efficiently and effectively, directly access our heart – and through it our spiritual heart – is to me the most important spiritual discovery of our time. I have seen this accomplished by thousands of people. They come from all different walks of life, and all different belief systems. It is simple. It is direct. It is effective. It is direct connection through your physical heart to your spiritual heart.

It is actually possible to watch this happen to your own heart in real time, using a device that HeartMath® developed, called the emWave®. This device shows, on a computer screen (or on a tablet or iPhone®), this amazing transformational change in your heart. You can watch your heart speeding up and slowing down, as the line goes up or down in real time. You can choose a heart feeling – a memory filled with a powerful feeling of joy or connectedness – and watch its effect on your heart. I have found it fascinating to watch my heart pattern (HRV) change as I enter into a powerful memory of a heart-filled moment.

The ability to monitor what happened in the brain and heart was instrumental in the researchers' being able to identify the steps we can take to implement this powerful shift that connects us with our spiritual hearts. They identified the steps, which I used, testing them on myself. HeartMath® has allowed me to share their techniques, expressed here in the language that I find most helpful for people. They developed these and other techniques to harness the heart's transformative power, testing and teaching them as practical tools for effective living. The HeartMath® researchers have tested thousands of people already, and there are many thousands more using the emWave to self-test.

I love the science. I love seeing the measured changes. But what I love most of all is the ability to actually do it, to make the changes in myself, to experience the amazing power and wisdom of my spiritual heart. My guess is that you will, too.

Chapter 12
Wisdom and Power

There is a part of these transformative experiences that we don't have the equipment to measure. It is the spiritual. This part of our nature that we refer to as spiritual seems to be beyond our scientific instruments. Some scientific experiments suggest that there is an element present in our lives that is beyond our capacity to measure or record, an element with great impact on our lives. They suggest an impact beyond what we are able to identify as our physical world. However, in fairness to our use of scientific information, inference is not proof.

Just because I really enjoyed learning about this, I want to share one of those experiments that deeply intrigues me. Researchers were looking into what they describe as our intuitive capacity.

A button was pressed, which was followed by a six-second time delay. After the six seconds, a computer would randomly select an image that was projected onto a TV screen. Most of the images were completely neutral, like an image of a rock. Some of the images were emotional, like a bloody knife. Each person watching the images was wired so that researchers could tell what happened in their brain, heart and other parts of the body.

Looking at the data from the whole group, the researchers could see that 4.8 seconds before the computer selected an emotional image, there was a response in the heart that sent a signal to the brain so that there was an anticipation of the emotional image. When I look at that data (and I am not a scientist nor a researcher), the experiment suggests to me that some aspect of ourselves that is outside of time and space connects through our hearts to tell our brains to prepare to handle emotional impact.

The only thing in my awareness that would fit that description is our spiritual nature. It is not limited by time and space. Its major point of connection to our consciousness is through our hearts. It directs our brains to help us respond to the challenging experiences of our lives.

Validation of your experiences with your heart as a transformative instrument will come from your own trial and application of this tool that activates your spiritual heart. Your life is the lab in which the presence and power of your spiritual heart is proven. What we do know from science is that we can measure its impact as transformative at our physical, mental, and emotional levels of experience.

Our examination here is not just a physical or mental one. When I heard my heart direct me to respond to my children differently at the bus stop, when I heard my heart direct me on the bridge to back up, I experienced much more than physical change or guidance. I felt something change *me*. It was not a thought to change. It was the experience of a change taking place within me.

I did not think about changing, and then make a decision. When I engaged the feeling from my heart-filled moment, it allowed the power of my spiritual nature to shift my physical systems, my mental capacity and my emotional experience.

Just as I had in the hallway with the doctor, I went from feeling fear to experiencing centered caring. In addition, I then "knew" the best response that I could make in that moment.

I know that this was not the body, although my body was affected. It was not emotional, although my emotions were affected. It was not intellectual, even though my mind was affected. I knew that I was in touch with a part of my being that was greater than my body, that was greater than my emotions, and that was greater than mere intellectual intelligence. I was in touch with a part of my being that I have come to recognize as my spiritual self. In those moments, this self demonstrated its power to me. It is not the power of being able to control things in the outer world. Rather, it is the power to transform our inner worlds. That power changed me, and transformed my experience, in those moments.

This power showed me what is greater than knowledge. This power showed me true wisdom. This power showed me hope in darkness, and it showed me the way through loss. It provided a way to interact with people, and it brought wisdom that guided me in relationships. These interactions connected me to the highest level within myself, and benefited the people in my life. In my first experience of this power at Kathy's death, this power changed me. It took me out of anguished emotional turmoil into forgiveness and peace.

What the research shows us is that specific changes happen. When you feel love, or a feeling associated with love, your heart, brain and emotions transform. These transformations cause other systems within you to up-level as well. The information I have studied demonstrated the transformation of at least six biophysical systems from incoherence to entrained coherence. This is an astounding level of transformation into a higher functioning within our biological systems.

Is it just a feeling – the feeling of love – that causes this change? Or is it that the feeling operates like a key that activates the spiritual power of our beings? I have worked with this for many years, because it is important to me to understand what is really taking place in our transformation. Again and again I have experienced personally – and heard from the experience of others – this transformative change that affects body, mind and emotions. At the same time, many people recognize this experience as the result of something more powerful than just positive feelings or good thoughts. It is the experience of the power of our spiritual hearts.

I have come to treasure my spiritual heart. It lifts my mind to its best functioning, but it is not my mind. It lifts my body to new levels of efficiency, but it is not my body. It lifts me to be a person living at a higher level, one who contains fulfillment and expresses my true values. It expresses who I really am.

On the cover of this book, I invited you to experience this amazing wisdom that can manifest your true heart's desires. It doesn't matter if that desire in your heart is for wealth, for loving relationships, for a great job, for a great career or for any other blessing, including enlightenment. This wisdom of your spiritual heart can guide you unfailingly, step by step, to the complete fulfillment of that desire. It will do that because that desire was placed on your heart by this spiritual self. Your spiritual nature is calling you to open to receive that good, that blessing, that potential experience of life – because that experience will be a very meaningful experience to you.

Knowing that your heart's desire is of true meaning to you, it calls you to fulfill those dreams. If you look at what your heart really desires, that desire is for an experience that blesses your life and fills it with some goodness or care for you or those you love. This is true of all our heart desires.

It is not true of our head desires. Many of our "wants" are simply our head's desires. Through the amygdala's emotional pattern, our brains try to compensate for fear, insecurity or sense of lack by projecting that having something or doing something will make us okay. Those desires can seem compelling for moments, but they are not rooted in who we are, and they soon fade.

Your spiritual heart's wisdom not only creates your dreams – it also guides you to the meaningful fulfillment of those dreams. It draws the opportunities for those experiences to you and opens you to receive their blessings. It is here to help you fulfill the purposes that are important to you, as a spiritual being having a human experience. I have heard many people share how following their heart's wisdom has brought jobs, relationships or creative opportunities into their worlds. I have seen so many lives fulfilled, just as mine was, by following this powerful wisdom of the heart.

Over and over in my life, I have listened to my heart, and found that its wisdom has guided me away from those endeavors that could not fulfill my dreams. It has unerringly guided me to step forward into the opportunities that would fulfill my heart's desires.

As a young man, I remember thinking that I enjoyed being a lawyer. I had a good income, and the legal work I was doing was interesting. Much of my efforts were focused on environmental issues that were new to the law at that time. They were exciting and challenging questions. I was surprised when my heart suggested that I should go to a ministerial school. I did not want to be a minister. I didn't like many of the things I associated with ministers. I liked the money, challenge and prestige of being a lawyer. However, I had a deep desire for spiritual understanding. In my free time, it was spiritual books (in addition to mysteries and thrillers) that I read, not legal ones.

This experience of my spiritual heart's guidance was new to me. It made very little sense logically, and my mind wanted to ridicule the suggestion. However, my family and my spiritual studies had spoken of guidance as a real thing, a valuable thing. I decided to pay attention to it.

In that experience, I began to discover the difference between the world of my thoughts and the world of my guidance. The major difference for me at that point was that what I recognized as guidance "felt" right. When I focused on it I had a "knowing" that it was what would be the best for me, and for my life.

I will admit that moments later my head would be back, wanting to argue with the guidance. However, the feeling of "rightness" was so compelling that I took the guidance seriously and began to explore that possibility.

I ended up following my heart's directive. It was very specific, and I found myself in a seminary enjoying spiritual study. When I graduated, I wanted to continue my spiritual learning, which I wouldn't have time to do if I returned to being a lawyer. As a result of my love of spiritual understanding, I followed my heart directive and went into active ministry, knowing that I could always switch back to the law.

What I found in ministry was uniquely fulfilling to me. This really surprised me. I found that I did not need to be like other ministers. I was working to help people live their lives with wisdom and love. That meant so much more to me than the law ever had. My heart guided me to a career that my head thought I didn't want. My heart guided me to deep fulfillment through this new career. My heart also guided me so that in the less remunerative profession of ministry, my family and I did not experience any lack – but rather we experienced abundance in every form.

Your true heart's desires include the short-term needs of releasing the emotional turmoil triggered by difficulties in your life. Finding peace in those moments, and connecting with your amazing wisdom, is a true desire of your heart. Your spiritual heart will make it happen when you use the access code.

As you meet life's experiences, your spiritual heart will also guide you to the intermediate steps to good jobs, to wise financial decisions, and to the relationships that fill your world with meaningful, joyous love. Follow your spiritual heart's wisdom, and you will end up with a life that is deeply fulfilling and a heart that is filled to overflowing.

Chapter 13
The Access Code

As we have explored these experiences, have you wondered about this access code to our spiritual hearts? The access code is really quite simple, as we saw while discussing the second of the steps of the Heart Wisdom Tool. It consists of the feelings that are connected in some way to the all-encompassing feeling of love, which we experience in our hearts.

It is not enough to have thoughts of love. We have to experience the feelings for the shifts to take place.

Let's explore these feelings a little more. We can also call them our heart feelings. They are generated by and experienced in the heart. Wherever you go in the world, if you ask someone about love, they will point to their hearts. I have never heard anyone say, "I love you with all my head."

I have worked with this code for over thirty years. I have taken the time to find it, study it, and learn how to use it. I've found ways to make it real in my life. I have also had wonderful opportunities to share it with others in keynote presentations, seminars, workshops, webinars, coaching and classes. As a result, I have been privileged to witness many people touch the positive feelings within their memories, and experience this same transformation. These feelings – all the feelings that are a part of love – impact us with their amazing, transformative power. They open us to the greater power of our spiritual hearts.

What the scientific research shows us is that when we feel the feelings that are a part of love, such as appreciation, care, compassion, joy or serenity, the human body is measurably changed. It is lifted into a higher state of functioning. These access code feelings are so powerful in their effect that the spiritual energy they open us to literally up-levels the efficiency, the intelligence, and the states of harmony and cooperation within the human body. These feelings activate our spiritual power, causing a transformation of physical, emotional and cognitive systems that elevate the functions of our body to a higher level of performance.

This shift is often described as a physical shift, because we are watching physical monitors when it happens. A physical shift does occur. When we measure the emotional and cognitive aspects of this, we see that measurable changes happen in these systems as well. As a result, we describe our experience as an emotional or a mental shift. While these measurable shifts do occur, they point to our capacity to access this spiritual power that causes these shifts, and which changes us in ways beyond what instruments can measure.

People activate the access code, these feelings of the heart, in a number of different ways. The easiest way for most people to activate a heart feeling (which we have been using here) is by memory. Some of these feelings we would not describe as love. We might call them joy, serenity, care, connection, success, gratitude, fulfillment or appreciation.

My understanding of love is that it is a very broad feeling. Just as sunlight hits a prism and displays the colors of the spectrum on the surface next to it, so love contains within it this multitude of positive, uplifting feelings. Each of them brings coherence to our heart's heart rate variability pattern.

I have had the delightful experiences of many people sharing their heart-filled memories with me: a grandchild opening its arms and running forward, calling "grandma"; a mother's first moment with her child as it is placed on her chest; a father's first time to feel his child give him a hug. They are moments on mountain peaks – at the ocean watching powerful, glorious sunsets – and moments in forests at the first light of early morning. All of these touch us: kittens playing, dogs bouncing in delight as we return home, and quiet moments, moments of strength or serenity. There are moments that have filled us with the most exquisite feeling – from our weddings and graduations, to moments when we simply delighted in the color, intricacy and fragrance of a rose. These are the moments when we feel our hearts. At these moments, through the miracle of feelings, we opened the door – and they can lead us to experience the power of our spiritual hearts.

Some of our most powerful memories come from family moments. These are the people we are closest to, and simple experiences can be powerful and profound. I have a special memory of sitting with Lisa when her little boy, Corwin, first discovered that he could feed himself with a spoon. He dipped his spoon into his pink yogurt, and occasionally a little of it ended up in his mouth. This delightful child and his squeals of glee, while he was completely covered with yogurt, brought us such joy. We laughed and shared this magical moment of happy discovery together.

I have a recent memory in which I read a story written by Lisa's twelve-year-old daughter, Fiona. It drew me in with complex characters and a twisty plot, and it wasn't finished – so I was left hanging and wanting more. I felt that I was given a sacred glimpse into the amazing talent of a young creative genius. I felt so humbled, appreciative and blessed. That exquisite feeling of being honored by spiritual insight into another person's soul touched me, and it is a feeling I can reach for and experience in the memory of that moment.

Some of our memories are of courage, some are moments of deep respect, some of patience that lifted us to a new level of strength. Some of our most meaningful heart-filled moments are our personal spiritual experiences. There are many memories and feelings of the heart.

There are also many feelings that are not from our hearts. Our fears, angers and frustrations, our hate and resentment, our impatience and judgmentalness are the protective mechanism of the amygdala in our brains, bringing up feelings that help us to separate rather than connect with others. These feelings prepare us to fight or flee, in order to survive our adversary. These feelings are the emotional reactions to patterns that are encoded in our physical and emotional structure.

These feelings are the ones that our hearts are often called upon to transform. These feelings are the ones that keep us from an active connection with our spiritual selves. Some of them become even more challenging, such as our feelings of indifference, or our feelings of burnout or despondency. Anyone who has had to deal with the experience of depression knows how debilitating that can be.

Even in depression and its related struggles, I have found that heart feelings are present, and that they can be activated. My good friend Toni has walked that difficult road. Again and again, as her depression threatened to overwhelm her, she had to reach into her heart and find her heart feelings. Each time she did, she found that she could take a step out of the dark hole that enveloped her. Each time she did this, she got stronger in this ability to get to her heart. I asked her how she uses her heart.

"Depression and its cousins, worry and anxiety, were standard for me throughout much of my life. Recently, while using the Heart Wisdom Tool around my feelings of being worthless, here is what happened: As I went through the first steps, and was able to get into my heart feeling world – in this case it was appreciation of my grandchildren – I asked my Spirit through my heart to show me what would actually work to unplug me from this old feeling nemesis. I asked very sincerely for my

Spirit's perspective, because I really meant that I was ready to be done with this feeling.

After only a few minutes of staying in the receptive mode, after asking my heart for a higher perspective, I was bathed in a soothing sense of inner peace. I was so still inside that nothing mattered but that beautiful feeling of total, quiet safety. And I knew that this place of safety was the answer to my worthiness question. It was not about being worthy; it was about feeling safe, so that I could just be who I really am in the eternal self I have come to know – the self who is anchored in my heart. The words that came up were "You are totally safe." I heard these words, right down to my DNA. And in that deep feeling of safety, worthlessness was completely irrelevant. I have committed to recalling and reliving that moment throughout my day, every day. I stop every three hours or so, go to my heart and just *feel safe.* I have noticed that I have more energy and enthusiasm for life – and my self-talk is seldom brutal. In fact, it's mostly gentle and kind.

My thinking mind would never have seen worthlessness as a *lack of feeling safe*. But now, because I asked my heart in a sacred communion with my spirit, it seems like common sense that feeling safe would dissipate old feelings of worthlessness. That's the power of the spiritual heart's wisdom. There would have been no other way for me to make this emotional shift except through my heart. And this way, I know I did it – nobody told me what to do – I did it as a sacred trust between me and my Spirit."

In many of the situations I'm sharing with you, the Heart Wisdom Tool is used right in the moment that the discomfort is taking place. When I was on the bridge, I used the technique right in that situation (well, after a few minutes of thinking of some colorful references to the person driving the Volkswagen). When I used it, my spiritual heart bailed me out of my emotional reaction. You may notice that a few of the examples take place some time after the triggering event.

When we get triggered in an emotional reaction, the reaction determines our response in that moment. We then continue to carry the emotional discomfort with us for quite some time. At least that is my experience, and that of many of the people I have worked with. I'm assuming that this is the same for you. Do you feel uncomfortable later in the day when something has bothered you? Perhaps you even think of it when trying to sleep at night?

Not everyone is that way. Some of us are great suppressors. We just ignore our feelings so effectively that we bury them in our body. Either way, the reaction is still there – and if we are honest with ourselves, we are still uncomfortable. This means, that in the evening (even if that evening is two weeks after the event), you can use the Heart Wisdom Tool to end your discomfort. Not only will it end your discomfort, you will then have a new relationship to the situation – one that is given to you from your spiritual heart.

If I use the Heart Wisdom Tool to transform my emotional reaction as soon as I become aware that it is still bothering me, it helps me then. Even though I might have spent several hours (or days) with the uncomfortable feelings, my spiritual heart can stop them at that point. I was excited to discover that if I keep using the tool when I remember to do so, my remembering gets closer and closer to the time that the actual triggering experience is taking place. Maybe, for a while, I will find that I remember a week later, when I can't sleep. Then it is only a few days after; then it is the same day. Pretty soon, it is only an hour later. It was that kind of growth that took me to the place where I could use my Heart Wisdom Tool to transform my reaction, when I was in the hallway with the doctor.

The more we use our spiritual heart, the more we remember to access it in the moment that the event is occurring. With the rush to the bus stop, I had not accessed my spiritual heart to transform the feelings of rushing and frustration that morning until we actually got to the bus stop late. By that time, the situation was difficult enough that I remembered to use the Heart Wisdom Tool and access my spiritual heart.

If you find you aren't using your Heart Wisdom Tool in a frustrating meeting or during a difficult conversation, don't be concerned. Whenever you do catch your upset, even long after the event, it is still very helpful. As you use it, you will find yourself remembering to use it closer and closer to the moment of the chaos, until, at that moment of need – such as in the hallway with the doctor – you can access your spiritual heart with its wisdom, its power and its love for you.

Chapter 14

Honest Heart

The guidance you receive from your spiritual heart is wise and effective. Its access code consists of feelings that are a part of the greater feeling that we call love. Referring to something like love often gives some people the impression that this wonderful guidance is going to be what we want to hear. It is going to feel loving and nurturing. I must admit that there are times that it does feel that way. However, I have had many times when there seems to be something else that shows up in the direction I receive from my spiritual heart. Often I am guided in ways that I don't want to go. I call this experience my "honest heart."

At those times, I experience my heart telling me to do something that I don't want to do. It is often telling me to take actions that my brain discarded because it had decided that the action was not kind, loving, or caring. Over time, I have found that my mind's evaluation of an action is often deeply distorted by what I find easy or convenient. My heart is honest with me about what needs to be done.

I had an experience like this when a couple I worked with for many years began to exhibit behavior that was destructive toward myself and the organization that I was responsible for. I was perplexed, and I did not know what to do. I met with them and attempted to work out our differences.

Prior to this situation, I'd had many experiences where my spiritual heart gave me the direction on how to successfully work out problems or conflicts with people. As a result, I was assuming that this particular situation could be handled with my heart guiding me in how to work everything out between us.

When I activated my heart and asked for its direction, I was surprised by its reply. It said to "Let them go – cease all contact." My heart told me that this was not my situation to work out with them, and it gave me an understanding of why that was so. My heart said that I should release them, and end the relationship.

I was convinced for a moment that my heart was wrong. I wanted to believe that I had the ability to work out a solution with these people. I cared about them, and this felt like failure. I went back to my heart and asked again. My heart's response was that my desire to try to work out the problem with them was my co-dependence. It directed me that my continued involvement, or that of my organization, would make the situation worse. I finally accepted my heart's wisdom. I trusted in its intuitive ability. I knew that it was being honest with me, whether I wanted that answer or not. I knew from years of experience that its guidance would lead me to what was most effective for me and for them.

As I went forward in the steps necessary to sever our relationship, I began to learn many things that helped me to see that my heart had been correct. It kept me from entering into a dialogue that would only have become more destructive for myself, and for many others involved.

When I thought of my resistance to my heart's wisdom, I realized that I knew I would be criticized for the actions my heart was guiding me to take. Part of my difficulty in accepting my heart's wisdom was not wanting to experience that criticism. Gratefully, I found that my heart was very honest with me, even though I did not want to follow that course of action.

I began to remember times when my spiritual wisdom took me to task for not facing or completing something that was uncomfortable. I would seek to avoid a decision that would result in having other people judge me. My heart would help me take the step, even if the result was unpleasant for me. It had often made me get honest with someone about a problem, instead of my beating around the bush or trying to avoid the uncomfortable situation that was before me. My spiritual heart asks much of me.

Your spiritual heart is highly intelligent. It works with much more than the data you are aware of in the moment. It intuits and understands your needs, and the needs of others involved. It doesn't pretend that you have skills that you don't have. It also knows your true power and strengths. It guides you away from what is not yours to care for, and guides you to engage effectively in what is yours to do.

Your spiritual heart is not only effective in the situations that show up in your current life. It is also effective in guiding you forward in fulfilling your life purpose.

I found that I often don't recognize that there is a greater purpose being accomplished in the situation before me. To my mind, the situations of my life often appear as just happenstance. However, when I activate my spiritual heart and call upon its guidance, my perception changes. I discover that I am weaving a tapestry that has a greater vision within it. This greater life tapestry, or soul purpose, is unfolding with the amazing help of my spiritual heart.

Your spiritual heart will at times give you direction that will feel uncomfortable. It may ask you to do things that you have avoided doing to keep from hurting someone's feelings, or avoiding a risk that you were reluctant to take. It may ask you to step into a life situation in a different way, one which feels unnatural for you. My experience has shown me that these kinds of directions from my spiritual heart – these actions I don't want to do, or are uncomfortable doing – are a genuine response of a greater presence of love flowing through my heart. I have come to trust them to be effective and important for my well-being.

I trust that you will find that these kinds of responses of your spiritual heart will empower and enhance your life. They are the result of a greater love guiding you forward effectively on your life purpose. They are your spiritual heart, lovingly being honest with you.

Chapter 15
Meeting Major Emotional Challenges

Let's journey into our access code once more, and expand its possibilities. The access codes we have explored so far are the feelings of appreciation, love, care and other feelings we can experience from our memories of times when our hearts were full. These amazing feelings that are our spiritual hearts' access codes are many and varied. The ones we have focused on are contained in the memories of moments when we were living our core values. These feelings are uplifting and positive. Their uplifting quality may be serenity, just as much as it may be passion or the uplifting quality of joy.

It is helpful to have identified a number of different specific memories to have available in activating your spiritual heart. You may want to identify memories of differing intensities as you create your heart memory repertoire.

I have identified a few very special, more powerful memories that I go to when I meet the greater challenges of life. I'm not thinking here of the everyday stuff, the frustrations, time pressures, irritations and hurt feelings that are common to life's everyday interactions. We can have lots of wonderful memories – from puppies and sunsets to a friend's hug – to use in transforming those daily reactive moments.

For highly charged or extreme situations, the memories I go to are so powerful that they overcome even the harshest reactions. I took some time to search through different memories to find a few that contained exceptionally powerful feelings. These are feelings so strong that by using them I can access my spiritual heart, even when my emotional upset is extremely strong.

One of the most powerful memories I have is of being in a small high school auditorium. I am sitting there, watching the play Camelot. The young actors are doing a great job – for high school students. As the play unfolds, its magic expands as it captures our awareness and draws us into its world, which becomes more real with each passing moment. The reason this play has become so powerful is the impact of the student who is playing King Arthur. When he is on the stage, we are seeing a true king – his power and his anguish are so real to us. When he sings, we enter into his world, feeling deeply the joy or sadness being expressed in his song. It is an amazing performance, and it opens my heart – affecting me in a whole new way as I watch this incredibly talented actor. His impact on me is profound – because this young man is my son. It is Peter. He is amazing. This boy I have known for eighteen years is now suddenly a person who has stepped into a new realm – and who has shown, at this young age, a mastery that few in life's long pursuit of such skill will achieve. My heart is open – it is filled – it lifts me to a very powerful place, a place of respect, of pride, of deep love and great appreciation. This is my powerful heart memory.

In the feelings of love and wonder that filled my heart in that moment, and in each moment that I remember it, there is enough power to free me from the strongest adversity. The feelings are so powerful that I don't even have to take a breath through my heart. The power of my heart opening pulls me into the deep, focused breath.

Your heart, too, has memories that are this powerful. People have shared with me moments from their childhood that are still filled with powerful heart feelings. Some of the memories were spiritual experiences; some were highly intense moments that occurred for them in what would seem to someone else to be an everyday interaction. Each person has spoken of how much more powerful and helpful these special memories were, once they identified them.

Many years after my heart had captured this memory of Peter playing King Arthur, I had an experience that required me to reach for the exceptional power of this memory in order to activate my heart. I was preparing to go out and share some inspiring thoughts with over a hundred people. The people had come many miles to connect with this wonderful information that I had for them.

Five minutes before I left the room to go down to the auditorium, a man opened the door to the room and stepped in. Even as the man entered, I felt that something was wrong. The man curtly told me to remain sitting, and he aggressively came and stood before me. From only a few feet away, he leaned over, pointing at me. With his face only inches from my own, he proceeded to angrily threaten my life.

He spoke of the pain he wanted to cause me, and how much he wanted to see me suffer that pain. He went on to describe, over and over in graphic detail, how he intended to kill me. He kept saying that he wanted to put a bullet through my brain. He was filled with a depth of raw anger and hatred that I had never seen in a human being before.

I was strongly impacted by his rage, the hatred that emanated from his being, and the raw violence and pain that he spoke of. Although I could not fully counter the impact of his hatred while he stood there before me, I did activate my heart – which guided me by telling me not to respond. My spiritual heart helped me understand that he was on the edge of acting out his desires, and that any response on my part could push him over that edge. After describing again how he wanted to kill me, and that it would be worth it to go to jail to do what he had described, he headed for the door. Turning one last time to growl out that he was deadly serious about what he had just told me, he left the room.

In the next few minutes, I would have to walk into a room of people waiting for inspiration. But the impact of the experience had shocked my being. This man's pure hatred heavily impacted me. It was difficult for me to pull my attention from that experience to focus on the people I was about to address.

The people in the auditorium, clearly, needed none of that. They had come to be lifted and inspired – not violated by the effect of that man's hatred.

So in that moment, I again called upon my heart. I needed the power of my spiritual heart to strengthen me and free me from the impact of the man's hatred. As I used the Heart Wisdom Tool, I was able to shift my body, shift to my physical heart, in a way that lessened my anxiety. I remembered memories of moments with my grandchildren. I could feel those memories while breathing through my heart. This was helpful, and the shock and anxiety I felt lessened.

However, I needed to be entirely free of the powerful reaction that this man's anger had produced in my system. The people I would address in a moment needed to experience real, tangible peace from my presence. I needed to go out and connect with them, heart to heart, responding to their needs – not mine. I needed the full power and presence of my spiritual heart.

I activated my spiritual heart again. I placed my hand on my heart, breathing deeply. I focused intently on the memory of Peter on that stage long ago. I reached beyond the impact of the man's anger, to the power of the feelings of pride, appreciation and love that my memory held. It was as though I was once again in that auditorium, watching the powerful performance of this talented young man. Those feelings of love and amazement were so strong that I could feel them change my body as my physical heart responded – becoming coherent, and uplifting my body.

As that love filled me, I began to experience more than the prior shift of my physical heart. I felt the transformative power of my spiritual heart. I called on it to fill me, to lift me. I called on it to take care of these people through me – and it did.

I walked onto that stage. When I looked at the people in the audience, I was excited about the wonderful inspiration I had to share with them. They did not need to learn of my difficult experience. The man had left, so I knew that what had happened could be handled later. At that moment, I got to experience being there, in my heart, with all of them. I felt love for them. I was grateful that I could choose the quality of this moment with them, and not give away my power.

After speaking, I did take time to allow myself to experience and be aware of the powerful impact that the man's hatred had on me. I gathered the support I needed, called the police, and took steps for healthy self-care, because I then had the time and opportunity to do that. It takes self-care, love and wisdom to deal with life's traumatic experiences effectively. We do not need to let difficult or highly impactful experiences remove us, or incapacitate us, from the demands immediately before us.

As I took my steps of self-care, I also focused my heart's intuitive wisdom on the man who brought such hatred into my world. As I very sincerely asked for a more effective response, my heart opened my understanding. I understood that he had no ability to control his rage or his hatred, once he opened that door. In understanding a little of his world, I realized what an effort it had taken for him not to act out, in that moment, the violence that he was imagining so graphically.

My spiritual heart guided me toward compassion and forgiveness. That inner peace is one of the most beautiful and meaningful gifts that our spiritual hearts can provide. It also brought clarity that while forgiveness could release me of my resentment, it did not change the need to effectively address the situation and the physical danger that it presented.

The demand immediately before me that day was both a personal and a professional one. Following a traumatic experience in your life, your need might also be professional – or it might be for wise action for yourself, your children, your friends, or for others around you. Your spiritual heart has this power to deliver you from the natural reactions of the mind and body so that your choice, not the actions of another person, will determine your responses.

Your spiritual heart can furnish you with wise daily guidance on questions before you. It can stop the everyday reactions of fear, anger, or insecurity that get triggered in our day-to-day interactions with others. Equally important – just as my spiritual heart had the power to free me from the extreme impact of the man's hatred and threats – your spiritual heart has the power to free you from the tyranny of emotions that follow your painful confrontations with others. It has the power to give you choice in how you respond, and in how you meet the demands of life that remain in front of you.

It is often these extreme situations where we need the greatest wisdom. Your spiritual heart has the deep, powerful wisdom that you need to meet every situation in life, from daily frustrations to the extreme happenings that can seem so overwhelming. This power and wisdom is always available to you in your spiritual heart. Here is an example.

Lani is a friend of mine who worked at a grocery store in our area. Lani is one of those people who lifts everyone's spirits by her very presence. I can't be around her without smiling and feeling better. The people she worked with – the employees, the employers and the customers – really enjoyed Lani's presence. Lani has a deep commitment to connecting to her heart. While she can seem almost ethereal because of her delightful outlook on life, she is one of the wisest persons I know.

One day when Lani went into work, her supervisor and another manager called her into the office and asked her about a simple transaction that had taken place a few days before. Lani went over the procedures she had followed, remembering them quite clearly and sharing them openly. In so doing, she realized that she had made a mistake in that process. It was a mistake that she had made once before, so, in going over the steps she had taken, she easily realized her error. As the managers pointed out her mistake, they suddenly appeared uncomfortable. They explained to Lani that the store's rules required that if a person made the same mistake a second time, they had to let that person go. Lani was suddenly being fired.

I'm sure you can imagine the strong feelings that would naturally impact Lani. She was suddenly without income. Lani lived very simply, and her income barely covered her life's expenses, which included caring for her children. Getting fired is an experience of rejection even in the best of circumstances. The mistake that Lani made was obviously, to her and to her managers, an innocent one. They knew that Lani was a person of high integrity. The firing had to feel very unfair.

As those feelings impacted Lani, she told me they almost took her breath away. Her hand went to her heart. With that simple connection, Lani brought her awareness to a memory that was deeply familiar to her. She remembered the powerful feeling that she was loved. This was a memory where she felt connected to her spiritual self, and to its wisdom that she knew had guided and cared for her all her life. It is a strong, vibrant feeling that she knows well. This feeling is strong for her in the same way that my memory of Peter's performance is for me.

As she called upon her spiritual heart, it guided her to acceptance. It opened her awareness to a number of parts of her experience. First, she became aware of the two people before her. She understood that they had no choice, and that this was a painful experience for them. She knew they really cared about her and did not want to be doing this. She realized that they had no choice – and simple acceptance released her from any futile emotional struggle. With that realization, she had access to her feelings of care for these people.

With this flow of awareness came a "knowing" that she was cared for. She knew that her needs would be met, and that this was only a change, not a lessening of care for her. These understandings were not just the mind's thoughts as it tried to deal with a hopeless situation. These were deep understandings that were lifting her. She was experiencing a strong awareness from an expanded perception that looked beyond that moment, in that room, to a greater reality that she had witnessed unfolding in her life over many years. From a moment of fully justifiable anxiety and defensiveness, Lani was in a clear experience of understanding this greater love and care for her.

With sincere care, Lani responded to the managers by saying she understood that they had no choice. She acknowledged their concern for her, and told them that she really knew that she was cared for and would come through this change just fine. She was able to affirm them and herself. A moment of victimhood that had been triggered by their pronouncement was vanquished by the greater power within her spiritual self.

Lani's gracious understanding of these two people and herself uplifted everyone, providing a view of a person connected to the power of her spiritual heart, a power that was greater than the momentary events of her life.

Lani told me, with delight, another understanding that followed those that I just shared with you. She said she remembered asking her heart about taking the job at the grocery store when it was first offered to her. At that time, her heart told her that she should take it. It further told her she would be there for two years. The day she walked out that door was two years and two weeks from the day she was hired. She understood that her spiritual heart had told her, even before she began, that it would guide her away to some other experience in her life at the right time. Within a few days, it did so in a very fulfilling way.

When Lani went home, she was not the victim of some company's inflexible rule. Rather, she felt free. She knew that she was an empowered woman, guided effectively into what would be an ongoing, uplifting adventure of love and care for her.

Several weeks after this experience, Lani told me with a smile that a customer from the store had approached her. The customer was a woman who had recently been injured, and who needed support to meet the challenges presented by her injury. Lani was hired to assist the woman. She found herself in a position that she enjoyed much more than working in a store. The position also provided a greater financial support for her life. This type of service, through personal care for others, was one of Lani's deepest desires.

Once you find this power, and learn that you can rely on the spiritual heart's wisdom, you will be able to use that beautiful wisdom to guide your life with a new sense of ease, through the experiences and the questions before you. This wisdom has changed my life in wonderful ways. I know that your spiritual heart can do that for you as well. Its amazing wisdom knows how to guide you to bring what your heart really desires into full expression. I hope you let it guide you to the true fulfillment of the deepest desires of your heart.

The Heart Wisdom Tool is at the core of a journey into one's spiritual self that holds infinite potential. How does one take that journey? The beginning is really quite simple. In whatever comes up in your life, put your hand to your heart.
   1 – Touch & Breathe
   2 – Remember & Feel
   3 – Sincerely Ask

From that place, you have the wisest guide on the planet, your spiritual heart.

Enjoy the amazing power and inspiring wisdom of your spiritual heart.

END

About this Book

In your hands is the access code to the highest levels of wisdom within you. That wisdom is deeply practical and makes a difference in your life in minutes. Your Spiritual Heart contains a powerful technique to access that wisdom based on the world-renowned Institute of HeartMath®'s scientific breakthroughs.

If you are frustrated because you can't get the right job, your career is stalled, or you haven't broken out of financial struggle, your spiritual heart has the wisdom to help you find and fulfill those heart's desires. If the loving relationship your heart desires has not come into your life, or the relationships you have are strained and becoming hurtful or unfulfilling, your spiritual heart's wisdom will guide you to the fulfillment of your heart's deepest desires.

Your Spiritual Heart contains the stories, the science and the technique to access to the amazing wisdom of your spiritual self. Your spiritual heart has the power to end your stress in a moment plus the insights to meet and exceed any challenge before you. Spiritual understanding and enlightenment are gifts of your spiritual heart. This book is an invitation to live at a whole new level of resilience and fulfillment. You can experience what it is like to step into humankind's greatest potential — heart-centered living.

About the Author

David McArthur's passion for understanding human transformation has taken him on this powerful path into the discovery of the spiritual heart. As an attorney his passion to help others took him into social service as an Assistant Attorney General in New Mexico working with environmental and consumer issues. His recognition of the power of the spiritual took him into spiritual study and ministry where he worked with individuals and groups of people in personal transformation for over thirty-five years.

Seeking the scientific principles of transformation drew him to the Institute of HeartMath®. At HeartMath he served on their staff for seven years including roles as a principle speaker and trainer as well as a director of their empowerment and religions divisions. There he discovered that through the spiritual heart one's desire for a better life becomes practical moment-by-moment transformation applied wisely in every day life.

Twenty years after he co-authored *The Intelligent Heart* with its revelation of heart intelligence, he shares with us the source of that wisdom. He has proven this source and its power in his own life and witnessed its transformation in the many thousands of people he has trained. From a lifetime of seeking comes a scientifically tested, spiritually powered guide to accessing your deepest wisdom and living a heart-centered life. More at www.accessingwisdom.com

60759898R00098

Made in the USA
San Bernardino, CA
12 December 2017